A GONDOLA
ON THE MURRAY

A GONDOLA
ON THE MURRAY

STEFANO DE PIERI

PHOTOGRAPHS BY JOHN HAY

ABC
BOOKS

The author and publisher gratefully acknowledge the following for their kind permission to reproduce poems in this book:

Peter Goldsworthy and HarperCollins Publishers for 'Tomatoes' and 'Ode to the Potato' from *This Goes with That*, HarperCollins, Sydney.

Phillip Hodgins and HarperCollins Publishers for 'Milk' from *Animal Warmth*, HarperCollins, Sydney.

Les Murray c- Margaret Connolly & Associates for 'The Broad Bean Sermon' from *New Selected Poems*, Duffy & Snellgrove, 1998, Sydney.

Published by ABC Books for the
AUSTRALIAN BROADCASTING CORPORATION
GPO Box 9994 Sydney 2001

First published in May 1999
Reprinted October 1999
First paperback edition May 2000

National Library of Australia
Cataloguing-in Publication entry
De Pieri, Stefano.
    A Gondola on the Murray: a passion for life, a passion for
    cooking with over 100 recipes.

    Includes index.
    ISBN 0 7333 0662 4. Hardback
    ISBN 0 7333 0876 7. Paperback

    1. Cookery, Australian. 2. Australians – Food. 3. Cookery,
    Italian. I. Hay, John, III. Title.

641.5994

Designed by Liz Seymour
Photographed by John Hay
Jacket background photo by Haynes Design
Illustrated by Adele Hann
Set in 10/12 pt Weiss by Seymour Designs
Colour separations by Finsbury, Adelaide
Printed in Singapore by TienWah Press

5 4 3 2 1

CONTENTS

ACKNOWLEDGMENTS

My wife Donata comes in on top of the list of acknowledgments as my best friend, which says it all. My in-laws, Don and Anna Carrazza, have made it all possible and I wish to honour them with this book.

My brother Sergio has come back to live in Australia where he continues to practise his art. He has been a source of inspiration for this book, which is about so many shared memories.

Various kinds of thanks and expressions of gratitude have to be distributed between Maggie Beer, Claude Forell and Joy Durston, Andrew Wise, Tony Tan, Trisha Welsh, Dugald McLellan, Terry Moloney, Brendan Moloney, Demetri Dollis, Susan Morris-Yates, and my staff at the Grand Hotel.

INTRODUCTION

When I was a child Australia played havoc with my mind. My older brother Sergio, the first of six children, was teaching organ music in Melbourne, playing frequently for the ABC, including its television channel, and keeping court in Carlton's now-fashionable Drummond Street. We were in Italy, still living in the same house of our ancestors; three families under one roof, without bathrooms and televisions but three separate kitchens. Fascinating letters came from my brother, with small stamps depicting various Australian animals. The letters actually smelled of the new world, and I knew then that all I wanted to do when I grew up was to go to Australia.

This burning desire was reinforced by the thirst I experienced in my teenage years for wild open spaces – an emotional reaction to the advance of industry, which radically changed forever my world in Italy – and by a strong dislike for the formal way in which Italian society was divided. At the top of the social pyramid were the untouchable political leaders, so well described by Peter Robb in *Midnight in Sicily*, a category intertwined with a sea of thieves, backroom dealers, corrupt officers of the State, deal hunters, anonymous directors in charge of enterprises founded on lies and political favours.

Those were the unfortunate years that saw the beginning of what became known as the strategy of terror. Italy was in the grip of dark forces, a kind of pre-Mafia coalition of conservative interests involving foreign powers, the secret service and fanatical right-wingers. All we had was a tin-pot Republic, a corrupt president who looked like a mouse and a Left opposition still obsessed by its own symbolism and driven by people who wanted the hammer and sickle to co-exist with the crucifix. (This president, a Neapolitan copy of President Marcos had his portrait in every primary, secondary and tertiary classroom throughout the country and the sight of him used to enrage me.)

I came to Australia, eventually, in 1974 on a comfortable, assisted Qantas passage and landed on my feet by falling under the protection and economic support of an extraordinary bunch of people; people who, in the old Left parlance, could have been described as 'intellectuals'. They pooled all their income into a single bank account and everyone could draw an equal amount each week for their basic needs. Greater needs – a house, a new car, an overseas trip – were the subject of lengthy meetings or major rifts.

This homegrown socialism worked very well for us, and for a long time too. It was a form of savings that all migrant families are used to; pure common-sense. That is how the Vietnamese community is getting ahead, for example. But we did not have the cohesion of a migrant family or the same needs. I lived comfortably with Bill and Lorna Hannan, one of the most dynamic couples I have ever met and a Melbourne institution, so I had everything I needed at that stage of my life and lots more. Actor Max Gillies, a member of the group, however, bought himself the entire collection of Bach's *Cantatas* while working in the USA. I don't think he ever declared the purchase to the group, which is perhaps why he kept it out of sight under the stairs of the Carlton house he shared with others. But I knew it was there.

Later my professional vagaries took me into politics and, on and off, into various professional and not-so-professional kitchens. For many years I wanted to be a cook, but instead I worked hard to become a member of the Victorian Parliament. When that attempt failed because of the machinations of the various ALP factions in the Victorian Labor Party, I took defeat in my stride and moved to Mildura, a town in the north-west of Victoria, with my recently married companion, Donata Carrazza. I knew that I would finally become a cook of some description. Donata's parents had long been in the hospitality industry and had recently acquired the Mildura Grand Hotel, a dream my wife's father had brewing in the back of his mind since he worked there as a very young porter in the 1950s.

His determination was provoked by a strange incident. The hotel manager once unfairly sent him home for the day, accusing him of breath that smelled of garlic. His indignation was genuine and justified because he does not like garlic very much, and his doting mother rarely and sparingly used it in her cooking, even though the family had come to Australia from the deep south of Italy where garlic is regularly used. Perhaps he had committed some other offence, but this story has gained currency over the years. There was no doubt, though, that the young Don Carrazza was going to take on the Grand – and its manager – for the next thirty years through a series of cafés and restaurants and licensed premises in a silent war driven by a combination of competitive spirit, southern Italian pride and youthful ambition.

If you have not been to the Grand or heard about it, you may ask what the fuss is all about. I assure you this is no ordinary pub. It is not that this hotel has preserved any of its former grandeur or has such features to make it stand out from other public buildings. But, rather like a pachyderm, it goes on forever, inside and outside and underground, a warren, a refuge, a home for many, and a church for others from the beginning of Mildura. The establishment for the well-to-do, it was dry until the 1920s, and when it got a liquor licence the management made sure that it would have a quasi-monopoly on the sale of beer. Imagine the quantities that have been through its taps and bottle shops! And the dry, hot climate was an attraction to thousands upon thousands of Victorian families that holidayed in Mildura and at the Grand especially. This is why so many people have stories to tell about the Grand. If only the Grand itself could tell stories – if only its walls had ears!

I have been at the Grand for the past eight years, and it is here that I developed my interest in cooking. I am of the school of the untrained, or the self-taught, and I rely very much on the memories of my past in the Veneto farm for the food I like to cook and eat.

The Municipality of Casier, where I come from, is not far from Venice – in fact, the River Sile, which flows through Casier, leads you into the lagoon of Venice and is still today a kind of waterway into the Serenissima. It is the memory of the gondola, that unequivocal symbol of Venice and its culture, applied here to this region of the Murray River that provides the title for this book.

The first time I visited Mildura was in the early days of spring. I was fascinated by the jacaranda trees in glorious bloom and the sheer quantity of broad beans growing between the vines. Les Murray's poem 'The Broad Bean Sermon' seemed entirely appropriate.

While fresh vegetables and extraordinary river fish such as the wonderful Murray cod are nearly always available in Mildura, many other ingredients have to be sourced from elsewhere. This requires tremendous initiative, good relationships with suppliers, faith in the transport system and ultimately the ability to improvise. The last is the quality I would like all home cooks to acquire: it is the shedding of fear, the courage to experiment, the exercise of judgement about which combinations give the best results.

It would seem to an observer just landed from Mars that the Australian media is more interested in food than almost anything else. Newspapers, magazines, radio and television programs provide a wealth of information about food and wine and in the last few years there is hardly a cuisine or an ingredient, however exotic, that has not been dissected, analysed and written about. There seem to be no secrets any more. For these reasons the environment has never been better for the home cook than the present. It is therefore a hard task to offer a cookery book when everything has already been discovered, when not a single, culinary stone has been left unturned.

My hope is that this immensely personal cookbook will fill tiny gaps here and there, and shed some light about one specific province of Italian cooking. I hope you will enjoy its discursive tone; for me food and politics are inextricable!

STEFANO DE PIERI

THE BROAD BEAN SERMON

Beanstalks, in any breeze, are a slack church parade
without belief, saying trespass against us in unison,
recruits in mind Air Force dacron with unbuttoned leaves.

Upright with water like men, square in stem section
they grow to great lengths, drink rain, keel over all ways,
kink down and grow up afresh, with proffered new greenstuff.

Above the cat-and-mouse floor of a thin bean forest
snails hang rapt in their food, ants hurry through several dimensions:
spiders tense and sag like little black flags in their cordage.

Going out to pick beans with the sun high as fence-tops, you find
plenty, and fetch them. An hour or a cloud later
you find shirtfuls more. At every hour of daylight

appear more than you missed: ripe, knobbly ones, fleshy sided,
thin-straight, thin-crescent, frown-shaped, bird-shouldered, boat-keeled ones,
beans knuckled and single bulged, minute green dolphins at suck

beans upright like lecturing, outstretched like blessing fingers
in the incident light, and more still, oblique to your notice
that the noon glare or cloud-light or afternoon slants will uncover

till you ask yourself Could I have overlooked so many, or
do they form in an hour? unfolding into reality
like template for subtly broad grins, like unique caught expressions,

like edible meanings, each sealed around with string
and affixed to its moment, an unceasing colloquial assembly,
the portly, the stiff, and those lolling in pointed green slippers…

Wondering who'll take the spare bagfuls, you grin with happiness
it is your health — you vow to pick them all
even the last few, weeks off yet, misshapen as toes.

LES MURRAY

WHAT YOU WILL FIND IN THIS BOOK

I have tried to follow the standard sequence comprising *antipasto*, soup, *minestra* or risotto, pasta, main course and dessert. One is not obliged to follow this order when organising an Italian meal – indeed serving all these courses would cause indigestion. However, in the old days of formal Italian dining, as many courses as listed would have been necessary for a credible *pranzo importante*, an important meal.

One of the first serious authors of a compendium of Italian recipes, Pellegrino Artusi, does not mention *antipasti* but recommends that diners begin with various *principi*, or starters. His starters are not as complex as the *antipasto*, which means 'before the *pasto*', the meal, not the pasta, which may or may not be part of the *pasto*. Today the *antipasto* has almost become a meal in itself, and often, at the end of an interesting *antipasto* my desire for the *pasto* proper has dissipated. Artusi goes on to suggest *minestre*, meat and fish dishes and does not seem to place a lot of importance on sweets at the end.

Much later, Luigi Carnacina, who became a dominant figure in food writing in the 1950s and '60s, the Thomas d'Aquinas of Italian gastronomy, provides this formula for a *pranzo*: a light starter, a soup, a fish dish, an offal dish, a meat course with a vegetable and a salad, and a dessert. His *pranzo* has at least six courses and one of these is nearly always of offal. Of eight sample menus he suggests, a wholesome six contain brains, kidneys, ox tongue, turkey wings and sweetbreads, while the remaining two contain anchovies and goose liver. Carnacina did not hesitate to assert the obvious – which is not obvious in Australia at all: what makes Italian cuisine different from other cuisines in the West is its extraordinary range of offal recipes.

For Carnacina it is this difference that elevates Italian cooking above the others. I do tend to agree with him, but hasten to add that Carnacina had not fully encountered Chinese and other Asian cooking in general at the time of writing – I suspect he would have been more cautious with his remarks if he had!

That aside, it is true that offal used to play an important part in Italian cooking and wasn't simply used to make the best of everything in a poor society. While that may have been the original reason, offal became part of the official good taste, the thing without which an important meal was incomplete. I mean, what is Italian food without *zampone*?

I am a little disconcerted by the horror the average Australian diner displays when encountering offal. I introduced some offal-based dishes at my restaurant, but soon enough, customers deserted me in droves. I persisted and continue to persist.

Another observation that is immediately obvious from Carnacina's suggested menus is the curious lack of any pasta dishes. He does not seem to regard them as important and places them, together with risotto, in the lunch menus, but even there, not with much enthusiasm.

There has always been a certain negativity towards pasta in the official circles. Marinetti, one of the fathers of the Futurist movement in art, regarded pasta as the reason Italians weren't a tough race, but he also had many other odd ideas. It is more likely that some writers saw pasta as a food of the poor, an item of little interest unless glorified, such as ravioli or *pasta al forno*.

Affectation also played a role. Smoked salmon was much more interesting than pasta; only later was it used for pasta sauces. It is only in recent times that I have heard opinion leaders talk with great solemnity about having a plate of spaghetti for lunch. This is not a bowl of spaghetti with some nondescript sauce placed on top: remember when that used to happen in Australia? The spaghetti, in this case, must be cooked perfectly *al dente*, to order, tossed with the best chopped tomatoes with a hint of garlic, basil, extra-virgin olive oil and a little parmesan cheese. To this base one may add the freshest shrimps, clams or mussels. Spaghetti served in this manner, followed by a light fish or meat dish with a salad and a good cup of espresso is more likely to be the typical contemporary lunch for many people, whether in business or at home.

An interesting curiosity: in the city of Venice, in the eighteenth century and before, certain State banquets had to be held on special occasions. The Venetians had a range of *antipasti* they called *ordover* (from the French term *hors d'oeuvre*). In the case of a recorded menu for an official State banquet for the ship workers these *ordovers* are: *arance belle grosse, una ciascuno* (beautiful big oranges, one each), salted tongue and Florentine *salame*, sponge cakes, ricotta, *savoiardi* biscuits and various pies and pastries. For the record, the hot dishes consisted of ten meat courses ranging from veal tripe and stuffed meat loaf, *galline alesse* and *colombi rosti* (poached hens and roasted pigeons) to poached and roasted veal and whole lambs on the spit. The meal would conclude with another ten dishes, cold again, with the inclusion of fruit and vegetables *per netarse a boca*, 'to clean one's mouth'. Listed among these courses we find artichoke, fennel and asparagus, and cheese and dry chestnuts which are to this day called *straccaganasse*, loosely translated as the chestnuts which tire your jaws.

Nearby, on the same day, in another room of the Doge's Palace, the nobility's bash displays a very similar menu except for the addition of natural oysters, various fish, more refined sauces and food of better quality. Other State banquets, says Massimo Alberini in his *Antica Cucina Veneziana*, do not vary a great deal, except for variations imposed by the seasons or religion. So, continues Alberini, on the fifteenth of June, on the festivity of San Vito and San Modesto, we find a very trendy *risi* (the Venetians talk about rice in the plural, as if they spoke of the single grains) with *pedocchi*, which must be mussels.

One can only imagine how different banquets must have been at the other end of Italy, in Palermo under Spanish rule, or in Naples for that matter. And what about the Vatican banquets? Were they nourishing themselves only on Mozart's *banchetti celesti* – the Commendatore, when he is invited to dinner by Don Giovanni, replies 'Where I come from we partake only in celestial banquets!' – or did all those men in red and purple eat something substantial?

I leave the answers to your imagination. One thing is for sure: the changes from century to century, from region to region, from class to class coupled with fads and fashions, imported affectations and, until not so long ago, religious rules – the *mangiare di magro* on all Fridays and during Lent when meat dishes were prohibited by the Catholic religion – make it impossible to simplify matters concerning Italian cooking.

Add to this the fact that not all Italians are good cooks. I have had many a ghastly meal in private homes where the cooks should have known better. Consider, furthermore, that Italians have, contrary to Australian opinions and Fellini's exaggerations, a pathological concern about *la figura*, the figure, so they eat like sparrows. I also believe that where incomes are limited as in the case of the majority who simply earn a monthly wage, food has to compete with other necessities. This may be why Italians consume mountains of cheap, frozen foods. *Il panino, la pizza* and *il gelato* (the roll, the pizza and the gelato) are other honourable exits from the commitment of a proper meal, especially among the young.

The formula *antipasto, minestre* and so on is borne of contemporary convenience; it exists for the sake of placing things within a traditional Western framework of entrée, main and dessert. I find this a very constrained way to eat, and have noticed how quickly we abandon this formula when we have Asian meals, especially when we share food in a group.

I much prefer to see exciting food on the table regardless of where it fits into our conventional classifications, in our obsessive pigeon-holing of things – the Venetians had cakes before dinner and the Chinese mix pork and prawns. The important thing is to keep an open mind and let good judgement, a sense of balance and good taste (three ways of saying the same thing) do the job.

ON THE USE OF POETRY IN THIS BOOK

Philip Hodgins is a great Australian poet and was a friend of mine. I was introduced to him by Dr Dugald McLellan, another friend, *bon vivant* and a world expert on Luca Signorelli, an important painter of the *Quattrocento*. I ended up sharing a house with Philip through yet another friend, Hartley Newnham, a famous counter-tenor and a lover of the arts. The house was located in Raphael Street, Abbotsford, in Melbourne, set against an elevated railway line, and a busy one. Many evenings were spent reading poetry, eating, telling stories, listening to Hartley on the piano, drinking – moderately – and occasionally aiming eggs at railway workers in the middle of the night. Workers repairing the line could only operate at night and they made more noise with their chatter than the hundreds of trains that ran from 5 a.m. to 12 p.m. Our vendetta against these enemies of sleep was to try to make a frittata on their faces. We delivered a few wet hand grenades but I doubt we ever hit anyone. Pity.

Philip was then an up-and-coming poet, and won the admiration of his peers. As I showed him how to make risotto, he would show me things he had written himself and often the works of other poets he admired, including Les Murray, whom he called the Supremo, though he was not always in agreement with Les's political views.

I remember Philip showing me a card he had received from the great man: it was a congratulatory note of some kind that indicated approval of his writing. Philip banged it theatrically on the table with a grin of satisfaction, like a confident chef who is proud to be highly rated by the best of food critics.

Philip enjoyed reading, among others, Robert Gray's poetry, whose clarity and ability to form images he loved, and Peter Goldsworthy, for his finesse, humour and charm. Later on Philip helped me set up a writer's festival in Mildura. I was finally able to meet with the many writers he had been reading to me over the years. Some of them have written beautiful poems about food, mostly about vegetables. (I suppose it's hard to write a poem about a bowl of soup or a braised shank.) It is my desire to share with the readers some lovely images of food that will relieve them from my prose.

Philip battled leukaemia for more than ten years until 1995. I am sure he would have had some fun writing more of his poetry for this book, and to select suitable poems by others had he stayed around a little longer.

From the kitchen of
a Veneto farmhouse some years ago

We have all been influenced in one way or another by our experiences with our parents. As a child I spent a lot of time talking about food and working to gather food or to organise its production with my parents. Being the last of six children, my father getting on with the years when I was growing up, I was fortunate to be caught, for a while, in a time warp and in a place which had not been affected by change in any way for almost a century. I grew up in a Veneto farmhouse, and that means existing on a fairly small plot, growing nearly everything possible for your own consumption. My father's age meant he was unsuitable for factory employment and too steeped in his old, semi-Luddite ways to introduce any risky developments into his life. In this traditional world – very similar in images to the film *The Tree of the Wooden Clogs* – life patterns were clearly defined: each month for each job, each month for a particular food to be grown, collected or consumed.

My father grew white asparagus, those that are grown inside mounds of earth and have to be picked before the sun changes the colour of the exposed tips. Asparagus was synonymous with spring, a bit of ready cash in hand, and some good meals.

When we wanted to sell some wine all we had to do was to hang a tree branch from another tree outside our house. This dead branch, *frasca*, signalled to passing traffic that they could come in and buy an *ombra*, a shadow. (This word has its origin in Venice: it is said that the wine seller used to follow the shade of the tower of St Mark to keep his wine cool. To this date, an *ombra* means a glass of wine and an *ombretta*, a smaller one.) The exposed branch is, apparently, an Austrian tradition, one that may have been borrowed during the Austro-Hungarian rule of northern Italy.

Workers on their way home would come into the shed, sit at a makeshift table, and order an *ombra*. I used to sell these *ombre*, as my brothers had before me. With *ombre* these fellows usually took some food: boiled eggs, cut in half, dressed with salt and pepper and, during asparagus time, some boiled asparagus.

I had a shoe box with a slit in the middle of the lid: this was my first till and I used to love to hear the sound of tiny coins rolling into it. With this education I should have become a businessman, but I think all these memories made me a hopeless romantic instead.

When I think of my mother, I always see her standing by the *cucina economica*, the wood stove with removable concentric rings so that a pot of any size sits easily on the fire. I see her stirring the polenta pot for over thirty minutes a day, a job she attended to for perhaps more than fifty years. I see on the stove, next to the polenta, a humble casserole of chicken or cuttlefish or, on a Sunday, a large pan of braised duck. Or I see her making a risotto with chicken broth and the livers and giblets of the same bird.

Sometimes, when in a less romantic predisposition and when I need to remind myself how lucky I am, I remember that our kitchen was only large enough to accommodate six at the table. Mother had to cook miracles when, after the slaughter of the pig at the peak of winter, she had salami, cotechini and sausages hanging from the rafters over the stove to dry. The constant drip of the salami water meant she had to do all her cooking while trying to avoid a shower of fat.

The day the pig was turned into pork, it was traditional to invite the neighbours over for a feast. The invitation was always reciprocated; it allowed everyone to relax and enjoy a lavish dinner, which was followed by a serious game of cards.

One year we had more neighbours-cum-guests than we could fit in the little kitchen with its shower of fat. It was promptly decided that we would dine in the only other space available for recreation in winter in the traditional northern Italian farm, the stable, complete with ruminating and occasionally defecating cows. The table was dressed with the best white linen, the glassware and crockery were those reserved for the important occasions. It was a memorable dinner for the number of guests made it serious and everything went well.

Such a dinner could begin with a large serve of rigatoni with a sauce of pork *ragù*. There would then be the mandatory risotto with pork and chicken mince and plenty of *grana padano*. A large salad of *radicchio rosso*, the best of all radicchio, would accompany fried pork hearts and livers, spare ribs, a roast of a part chosen by the *salumiere*. Other bits of meat – like duck or guinea fowl were the choice of the cook. A light-style merlot would accompany these meals. Uncle Gigio, however, had a respectable patch of Barbera which made a better wine than most. In these days of lean pork it is hard to imagine such a calorie-rich dinner, but those flavours left in my mind an indelible memory of taste.

It is harder than ever to speak of taste: to say that one is after taste is to state a truism – who would say that he or she is not? And yet it is precisely in the space between the said and the unsaid that the very notion of taste is lost, and in a big way. How else can we explain many a restaurant and even committed home cooks preparing bland meals?

La cultural del gusto, the culture of taste, is not important to many people as I see it.

The search for the latest technique, ingredient or combination of ingredients seems to me to take precedence over what the food on the plate should taste like. Very little of what can be described as challenging food is either presented to the average diner or cooked by the average household. How often have I heard the phrase 'There was nothing wrong! It just wasn't my type of food.' This would have to be the most myopic of all judgements, for it denotes a lack of curiosity and an obstinate will to remain in the territory of the safe.

Part of the problem was illustrated with perfect clarity by Terry Durack in an article in the February 1998 issue of *Vogue Entertaining* magazine. He states that too many restaurants are caught in the 'dumbing down' syndrome. This is a condition whereby everything is reduced to minimum common denominators – not to be confused with simplicity – and a flattening of the range of possibilities. So down we go to the omnipresent interaction of char-grilled (why not just grilled?) baby octopus with sweet chilli sauce, and an Asian-style salad. This is an outright abuse of the freedom of

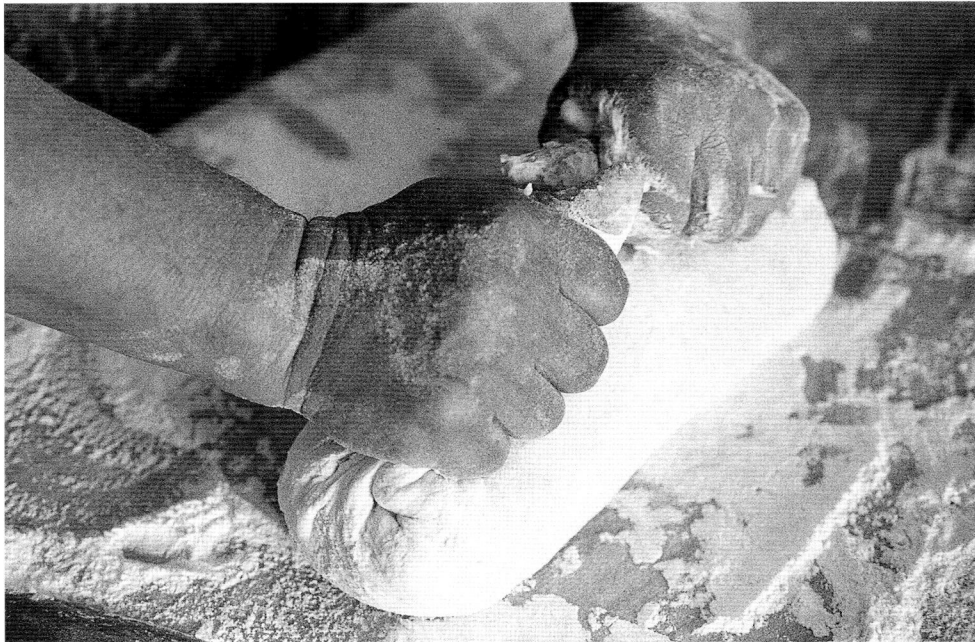

expression that we possess in Australia by virtue of our multiculturalism. It is paradoxical, but the very thing that advanced food knowledge – multiculturalism – may well be the cause of the decline of food in Australia, especially if cooks stay with the safe dishes they borrow from everywhere rather than explore more challenging ones. I am not sure about this thought; only time will tell.

Worse still, there is a child in our collective palate who refuses to grow up. This child is still screaming, loudly, for cappuccino at the end of a very long and satisfying meal. How can we allow ourselves to do this? Where is the decorum in a quick lunch that consists of cappuccino and minestrone at the same time? Where did this trend, whereby people have to get a fix of five or six cappuccini or 'latte' a day, at the expense of other, more suitable, drinks come from?

We seem to violently change mood and swing from one excess to the next. We go from men wearing shorts like little kids to men in adult clothes drinking numerous coffees per day, mostly with sugar. What does that say about our palate?

Those of us who really care about food and do not wish to see Australia taken over by interminable suburban avenues of fast-food outlets or their trendy equivalent – the caffé – should be vocal about what we eat and drink, how and when. It would be healthier and wiser, in my view, if, for example, people were permitted to enjoy a small glass of a low-alcohol bubbly wine with a nice crostino for a late-morning break rather than a watery, hot, sugared cappuccino that looks like a souffle with a terrible piece of toasted white bread. And when I say one small glass, I mean one small glass. Not two. Just one, without jokes, innuendos and sense of illegality; one with dignity, and as a matter of fact.

GLI ANTIPASTI
AT THE BEGINNING

Besides the traditional, well-known *antipasti* such as prosciutto and rockmelon, there is no limit on the number of *antipasti* one can create. You can go as far as the imagination permits.

A good *antipasto*, in the traditional context, is only meant to whet the appetite in a gentle and seductive manner. However we have come to eat so many different *antipasti* in Australia that each creation can, conceivably, be treated as a small entrée. It is possible to serve the dishes in this section in succession, like a Chinese *yum cha*, especially for an informal Sunday luncheon.

Some of the *antipasti* I have chosen reflect the products of the Sunraysia district, but most of these ingredients are available all round Australia.

Peperoni Arrostiti a Più Colori (page 32)

Insalatina di Finocchio e Arance con la Sasizziella

FENNEL AND ORANGE SALAD WITH SASIZZIELLA

A refreshing salad made with the almost-seedless naval oranges that is a healthy starter or a good salad for any occasion. Sasizziella is salt-cured tuna from Sicily. It can be purchased in small, easily sliced blocks from specialist Italian food stores.

Serves 4

PREPARATION TIME: 40 MINUTES

8 thin slices sasizziella, marinated in extra virgin olive oil

3 navel oranges

1 large bulb fennel

salt

lemon juice

olive oil

freshly ground black pepper

Select a crisp fennel and remove its outer leaves. Cut in half and trim away the hard core. Rest each half on the cutting board, face down, and slice finely. Sprinkle a teaspoon of salt on the fennel and toss on a large plate with a few drops of lemon juice. The salt will extract the water from the fennel and soften it in about 30 minutes.

Marinate the sasizziella in the oil for at least 15 minutes.

Peel the oranges with a sharp knife and make sure there is no pith left. Remove segments by cutting into the orange on either side of the membrane. Squeeze the juice from the membranes over the segments to keep them moist.

Before serving, tip out the water released by the fennel, add the orange segments and enough olive oil to coat the salad. Grind some pepper over the salad and add the sasizziella.

Insalatina Fredda di Cozze, Pomodoro e Finocchio
SALAD OF MUSSELS, FENNEL AND TOMATO

Aim for subtle and clean flavours when preparing this salad. If it is hard to find good tomato and plump fennel — technically the seasons do not coincide — replace the fennel with tender green beans cut in half or, alternatively, discard the tomatoes. You can use even supermarket tomatoes if you use only the shells. Cut the tomatoes into small wedges and with a sharp, small knife cut away the seeds, leaving only the flesh attached to the skin.

Serves 4
PREPARATION TIME: 40 MINUTES ALL UP

I medium-sized fennel

lemon juice

2 kg (4 lb) black mussels, beards removed

4 teaspoons extra virgin olive oil

I small, red chilli, seeds removed
and finely sliced

5 parsley stalks

4 cloves garlic, crushed

125 mL (½ cup) white wine

4 tomatoes, seeded and flesh cut into strips

4 teaspoon chopped Italian (flat-leaf) parsley

extra virgin olive oil

extra lemon juice

black pepper

Slice the fennel as thinly as possible and salt lightly. Sprinkle with a few drops of lemon juice and allow to stand for about 30 minutes.

To cook the mussels, heat olive oil in a large saucepan with the chilli, parsley stalks and garlic. When the ingredients are sizzling drop in the mussels at once, taking care to avoid any splashing of oil. As soon as the temperature is up again splash with white wine, place a lid on the pan and cook for a couple of minutes or until the shells begin to open. Remove the mussels as they open: there is nothing worse than rubbery, wrinkly mussels that are overcooked. Extract the mussel flesh as soon as possible and set aside.

When you have opened all the mussels strain the liquid into a bowl and rest. The grit will sink to the bottom. The remaining clear juices can be used to flavour a seafood risotto or other fish preparations. If you are not using the mussels until later use the juices to keep them moist.

To assemble, toss mussels, drained fennel, tomato and parsley — I prefer to tear parsley with my hands even if the result looks a bit rustic — with olive oil, a touch of lemon juice and black pepper.

Serve with some crusty bread rubbed with garlic and olive oil.

INSALATA DI GAMBERI D'ACQUA DOLCE
YABBY SALAD

These wonderful freshwater creatures used to live in the rivers and channels of northern Italy, where some restaurants specialised in yabby dishes. Now nearly extinct, yabbies are something Italian children do not even know exist and will never experience the pleasure of fishing for them.

As long as there are dams and creeks in Australia I think yabbies are going to continue to be available for home use. Many yabby farms now provide this delicacy in great commercial quantities nearly all year-round.

Most yabbies are already cooked when they reach the shops. So many people I know are startled when they taste a yabby cooked in a good vegetable stock and are delighted to eat it dressed in olive oil. It's worth trying to get them fresh and to cook them yourself.

Serves 4
PREPARATION TIME: 30 MINUTES

20 large, preferably uncooked, yabbies

1 onion, rougly chopped

1 stalk celery, chopped

5 peppercorns

5 parsley stalks

1 cup (250 mL) white wine

1 bay leaf

salt

1 bunch rocket (arugula) and a few other salad leaves of your choice

1 ripe avocado, sliced

12 segments grapefruit

olive oil

lemon juice

salt and pepper

To cook the yabbies, prepare a small pot with water flavoured with onion, celery, peppercorns, parsley stalks, white wine, bay leaf and a large pinch of salt. When the water comes to the boil drop in the yabbies and cook for 5 minutes or so. Yabbies, like most seafood, are better if a tiny bit undercooked rather than over-cooked: they will stay moist. Remove and let cool.

To assemble, remove yabby tails, peel and pull out the intestinal tract and discard. Toss the tails with green leaves, avocado and grapefruit, and dress with olive oil, lemon juice, salt and pepper. Pass the heads and claws around separately with some nutcrackers.

ASPARAGUS

If I were to single out a sweet, childhood memory, I cannot go past picking asparagus with my father in the early hours of the morning in late spring. (Being white asparagus we had to pick them before the tips changed colour.) The poppies would all be out in the wheat paddocks, the dew not yet so cold on our bare feet, and the first poplar mushrooms were just beginning to form. In the distance, the sound of my brother practising Chopin for his exams.

Philip Hodgins and I used to talk about why childhood memories seem so sweet and to what extent memories influence art. His favourite memory was standing barefoot in warm cowshit on a cold day. (His parents were dairy farmers in Shepparton, central Victoria.)

Our asparagus were grown in mounds of earth that went for some 2.5 kilometres. They were cut from the base with a long and sharp knife, washed, bundled up in different sizes and trimmed at the bottom for a nice, uniform base. The bundles were tied up with the attractive and inexpensive skin of the long mulberry branches, and the leaves were fed to the silk worms.

Then my father and I would go off to the market, with me sitting on the bar of his bike. For years and years the stall of Anselmo and Amalia, behind the Square of San Vito in Treviso, had been taking our asparagus. Then father and son would go to El Canevon, a wine bar, where I was allowed to taste sweet white wine served with *biscotti*.

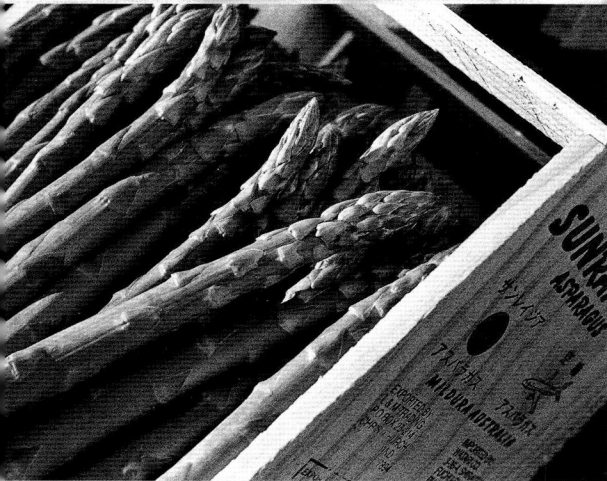

Wild asparagus grow in Mildura along the channels or the roadside. How they got there in the first place is recounted by Alice Lapthorne in *Mildura Calling* in 1946:

At this stage cases of typhoid fever were reported, resulting in campers being ordered off the flat to their building sites in the township. Dr Abramowsky, grandson of a governor of Warsaw, had bought a residential block at the corner of Ninth Street and Deakin Avenue, but beyond the fever outbreak found little to do in such a healthy climate, so devoted himself to the spreading of the doctrine of a fruit and vegetable diet. With pockets full of almonds, raisins and dried figs, which he gave to his juvenile friends, he cycled about the district telling people how to keep fit. He grew vegetables, kept bees and planted 20 acres of asparagus but could not cultivate local interest in this edible plant so, as the story goes, he threw some berries into the channels: these were distributed by the irrigation waters, hence the asparagus which now grow wild along the headlands of blocks all over the settlement.

By the 1930s matters had changed, as shown by the following letter from the Victorian Department of Agriculture to Mr J. Castle of Red Cliffs. A granddaughter of Mr Castle, Mrs Ruth Penny, a proud local, showed me the letter:

Melbourne, 29 November 1930

Dear Mr Castle,
I have to advise you that the case of asparagus consigned to me for a test of suitability for canning arrived in excellent condition, and I have to congratulate you on the excellent manner in which it was selected and packed. The asparagus has since been canned by the Australasian Jam Co., South Yarra, and their report is that, apart from excessive thickness of the skin, the sample was a perfect one for canning.
    As a result of this test I am interesting this firm in the establishment of a canning plant in Mildura.

Kearney
CHIEF SCIENCE FIELD OFFICER

If only one could establish a factory with a box of asparagus!
    It is also interesting to note that a Mr Frank Minter decided to plant asparagus in 1927. This was the white variety and was packed in attractive wooden boxes with layers of grass to keep it fresh on the trip to the Victoria Market in Melbourne.
    There are now eighty-five asparagus growers in Sunraysia. The Ida Lea variety is now planted extensively because it is best suited to this climate. It is harvested from July to December, a very long time indeed.

UOVA E ASPARAGI
ASPARAGUS AND EGGS

When I was growing up, asparagus seconds which were not good enough for the market were eaten at home as a salad with eggs, used as a base for risotto, or stewed with tomato and as a pasta sauce.

Serves 4

PREPARATION: 20 MINUTES
(MAINLY FOR TRIMMING THE ASPARAGUS)

1 kg (2 lb) fresh asparagus
(avoid limp-looking ones)

4 hard-boiled eggs

olive oil

lemon juice or red-wine vinegar

salt and pepper

Trim the asparagus by cutting off the hard ends, if any, and remove the last bit of the skins. (This is more a visual thing than a necessity. Try one or two asparagus without cooking to see if there is any grit hidden inside the leaves — when it rains water spurts sand up against the asparagus and their leaves trap in the sand. If gritty, remove as many leaves under the tip as you can. It is a boring job, but I hate grit in my mouth.)

Once the asparagus is ready wash and plunge them in plenty of boiling salted water for no more than 1 minute. Remove and plunge into cold water. Add some ice to help cool the asparagus quickly.

Place the asparagus on a serving plate, crush the eggs with a fork and dress with olive oil, lemon juice or vinegar and salt and pepper to your liking.

Asparagus with Poached Egg and Prosciutto (page 31)

Frittata di Asparagi Selvatici
WILD ASPARAGUS FRITTATA

Elizabeth David talks about bruscandoli in one of her celebrated books. Some misinformed person told her that they were wild asparagus — her subsequent research showed that they were some kind of wild hop. I know them well because they are among the first things to grow in northern Italy, along with the wild violets, in spring.

Trust Elizabeth David to write about bruscandoli! There seemed to be no secret safe from her inquisitive mind. Bruscandoli, I thought, was my secret. As a child, gathering bruscandoli was my favourite occupation after school and the adults were always appreciative of my efforts. Wild hops are pink when they first appear and turn green a little later. They are beautiful to see and stir in me the ancestral urge to gather food. They are also the base for the ultimate risotto or a great frittata.

In Australia, where bruscandoli do not exist, wild asparagus make more than a decent alternative. I have seen them in city shops, although very rarely. If you live in the vicinity of anyone growing asparagus you are likely to find them because asparagus seeds travel easily and grow almost anywhere.

Serves 4
PREPARATION TIME: 15 MINUTES

16 stalks wild asparagus,
or of the usual variety

butter

olive oil

8 large free-range eggs

4 tablespoons grated parmesan cheese

4 tablespoons cream

salt and pepper

Preheat the oven to 180°C (350°F)

Trim and wash the asparagus and cut into small pieces. Fry in butter and a touch of olive oil, gently, until soft. (Use a pan that you can place in the oven.)

Crack the eggs into a bowl, and mix with parmesan cheese, cream, salt and pepper. When well mixed pour over the asparagus. Stir gently with a fork over a low flame — be careful not to damage the bottom of your pan — until you see the bottom of your frittata beginning to form.

At this point place the pan in the oven where the frittata will cook in about 10 minutes. Try not to overcook. Remove from the oven, run a spatula around the edges of the pan, tip it upside-down on a tray and then upside-down again onto a suitable plate.

All frittatas can be done in this manner. Make sure that you prepare the base properly. Cook it well so that you get a maximum integration of flavours.

Asparagus with Poached Egg and Prosciutto

Serves 4

PREPARATION TIME: 20 MINUTES
(MAINLY FOR TRIMMING THE ASPARAGUS)

1 kg (2 lb) fresh asparagus,
trimmed and washed

4 eggs

unsalted butter

lemon juice

black pepper

best-quality parmesan cheese, grated

4 thin slices prosciutto

Plunge the asparagus into plenty of boiling salted water for no more than 1 minute. Remove and keep warm.

Poach 4 eggs, then arrange on top of spears of asparagus on individual plates. Dress with a combination of shavings of unsalted butter, a little lemon juice, black pepper and shavings of parmesan cheese and a thin slice of prosciutto, which will wilt in the heat of the asparagus and the egg.

Fave Fresche e Pecorino
BROAD BEANS WITH PECORINO CHEESE

Renowned chef Stephanie Alexander wrote about a wonderful dinner at Chez Panisse restaurant in the USA which began with fresh broad beans (fava beans), oil and sea salt flakes. I admire the courage of anyone who puts fresh vegetables in front of diners! This particular dish must perplex people who are not used to eating fresh broad beans, so I thought I may add my voice in support of such an excellent idea.

There is no actual recipe: get hold of very fresh broad beans, those that have not hardened but are not too young as they have little crunch or flavour. Obtain some best-quality pecorino cheese — taste before you buy — and a good bottle of light Chianti wine. Sit down with your friends and eat the beans with slivers of cheese, wine and sprightly conversation.

If you are bold, serve the beans in a rustic basket at the end of a spring dinner with the block of pecorino on a cheese board in the middle of the table.

Peperoni Arrostiti a più Colori

TRIO OF ROASTED CAPSICUMS WITH GARLIC AND ANCHOVY PASTE

*This is not an original recipe but one worth repeating. It is also an excuse to use
Western Australian anchovies — you won't find much better.*

Serves 4 (with some leftovers)

PREPARATION TIME: 30 MINUTES

3 red capsicums (bell peppers)

3 green capsicums (bell peppers)

3 yellow capsicums (bell peppers)

slices of Italian-style crusty bread, or slices
from a breadstick

1 clove of garlic

olive oil

12 anchovy fillets

2 cloves garlic, crushed

½ cup parsley, basil or mint, finely chopped

Preheat the oven to 180°C (350°F).

Wipe the capsicums clean and place them on a baking tray in the oven. When the skins are blistered on one side turn them to ensure even cooking. Do not overcook or the flesh will be mushy.

Remove from the oven and when cool peel, remove seeds and cut the flesh into strips.

Grill the bread on both sides, rub with garlic and drizzle over some olive oil.

Place capsicum on an attractive platter with the bread.

Place anchovies and garlic in a food processor and with the motor running, pour as much oil as necessary to obtain a spreadable paste. After spreading the paste on the bread, sprinkle with parsley, basil or mint.

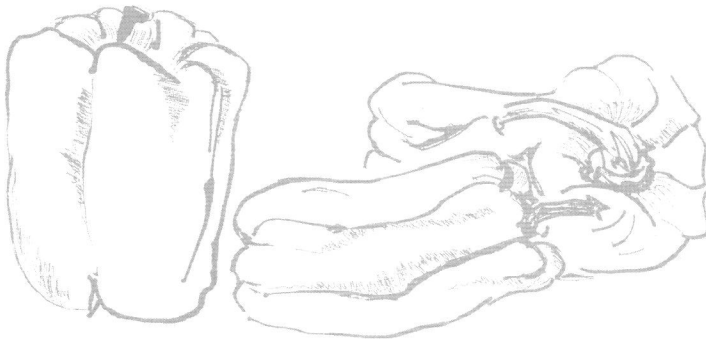

Peperoncini Ripieni di Capperi e Acciughe
SMALL ROUND CHILLIES WITH CAPERS AND ANCHOVIES

This preparation requires the small, round chillies called Chilli Ball. They are the size of a twenty-cent piece and are not too hot. You also need the best capers, and these can be purchased from specialist shops. I prefer the salted variety — I wash the salt away, dry and place them in a jar with oil.

It is best to prepare a batch rather than a small quantity. These chillies are gorgeous by themselves or with meats that have been poached or steeped. I love serving them with Pollo in Bianco alla Maniera Cinese (see page 42) instead of the traditional soy sauce dipping sauce.

Makes 20–30
PREPARATION TIME: 1 HOUR
20–30 chillies
1 L (4 cups) olive oil
small capers
20–30 small anchovies

This is what you do: with a small knife cut a hole in the chilli and remove the stem and seeds — all the seeds.

In a small pot, heat the oil to a point where it is hot but not smoking. Turn off the flame or remove from the stove. Plunge the chilli at once and let them steep in the oil until cooked and cool. In this manner you will not scorch the skin of the chilli and they will not look wrinkly. If your chillies are red the skins will look glossy. If green the skins will turn the colour of green olives.

Carefully fill each chilli with 3 or 4 capers and 1 anchovy. Place the filled chillies in a jar and cover with the same oil in which they have been cooked. They are not for keeping because there are no preservatives in this preparation. The oil should also be used quickly because it will spoil having been in contact with the chillies' residual water. Use it in pastas or to dress roasted capsicums.

OLIVE OIL

The combination of olive oil with lemon juice, parsley, garlic and chilli would have to be regarded as one of the most important group of flavours in contemporary Italian cooking. And as you have gathered not only from this book but from almost daily experience it is hard to cook in modern Australia without reference to olive oil. I now find that a number of professional chefs actually include olive oil in Asian-inspired recipes which traditionally use various seed-derived oils or palm oil.

Not that it has always been that way. When I was growing up in the Veneto we did not use olive oil at all. The cuisine of the north employed pork fat, butter — always, even to braise *osso buco* — and vegetable oil. When we speak about Mediterranean cuisine and diet we should automatically exclude the cuisine of northern Italy, which should be called the cuisine of butter!

I think I first had a taste of olive oil when I was twelve, perhaps even older. My brother Tony had obtained some of this exotic condiment from some truck drivers from the Puglie region in exchange for some wine. I was immediately taken by the colour and the intensity of flavour of this oil, which suited so well our green radicchio salad.

But for all my liking of olive oil it wasn't until recently that I fully understood how it is made and what one should look for in the process. This happened when a friend of mine, Gianni Grigoletto, also from Treviso, and a resident of Wodonga, turned up on my doorstep with a new piece of equipment imported directly from Italy. He said, 'I hope you have some olives because I want to practise making olive oil with my new machine.' Gianni had travelled from Wodonga to Mildura with an olive oil-making machine and a generator on the back of his truck in the hope of finding some olives — the ultimate romantic gastronome!

The machine, manufactured by a Tuscan company, is worth mentioning. It represents a small investment that enables people with a non-commercial olive plantation to make their own oil. The machine is big enough to keep pace with several pickers but small enough to be affordable, somewhere between ten and twenty thousand dollars, depending on the number of accessories.

The one-block unit incorporates a hammer crusher, a cold paste homogeniser and a continuous centrifuge separator. In other words, the olives are crushed cold, without the addition of water, and that paste is stirred continually before being channelled into the centrifuge which separates the oil from the rest. Oil comes out slowly but fairly clean on one side and the waste — including water, the arch-enemy of oil — from the opposite side. The simplicity of this equipment is staggering and perhaps a bit of an anti-climax.

Some olives for Gianni I did have. Luckily, in an off and very dry year I had a few trees to offer him and the process of experimenting began in earnest. There is very little in the world that is as exciting as picking your olives and seeing the oil come out within a few hours! And although we picked very green olives and the yield was very low, the oil was fantastic.

Oil made with freshly picked olives that have not oxidised or fermented has a distinct flavour. The cold pressing and the separation without any extra aid to increase the extraction ensure that the oil tastes like it should, a fresh olive, with a distinctive slightly bitter character that is frequently absent in most Australian-made olive oils that I have tasted so far. At the risk of making enemies — even among my friends who produce commercial quantities of olive oil — I will say that most of the existing presses in Australia tend to make all oils taste much the same.

Furthermore, merchants and providers are not very discerning about what they sell. Some of them are not even aware that olive oil should be dated, because it is no longer very good after twelve months. Some do not know how the oil was made and where. This general lack of education is producing olive oil consumers who do not know how to distinguish between an olive oil which is rancid and one which is fresh. Above all, consumers do not yet know what to look for in an olive oil and how to assess what they should really pay for it.

I have given a great deal of thought to these sentences. I have looked at them for the best part of two years, agonising about offending people who have pioneered olive oil in Australia, asking myself whether I am biased or in any way injudicious about what I have written. And I have decided to stand by what I believe until we improve our knowledge of which varieties work best, and where, and our technology and know-how are improved.

OLIVE SCHIACCIATE
CRUSHED OLIVES

*I have access to vast quantities of olives, but so have you, especially at Easter time, when the first green
and plump olives hit the metropolitan markets. These crushed olives are fun to prepare and make great snacks.
As it takes about ten days to complete the project, do not bother with less than 5 kilograms of olives.*

Makes 5 kg

PREPARATION TIME: 2 HOURS
ZMARINATION TIME: 10 DAYS

5 kg (10 lb) green olives

salt

water

5 whole fresh chillies

5 sprigs oregano

10 whole garlic cloves

Hit the olives with a mallet to split them. Remove the pips. This is a messy job, so wear an apron and gloves unless you are prepared to have black fingers for a few days. Place all the split olives in a tub with enough water to cover. The water should be salted much like sea water.

Change the salted water every day for a week. On the seventh day you will notice the bitterness in the olives about to go. Keep going for three more days. At this point, drain and dry the olives. (Their colour will have changed.)

Place in sterilised jars with chilli, oregano, garlic and a little more salt. Fill with olive oil and wait for two weeks: they will be ready for your *antipasto*.

These olives are not for keeping: they will become mushy after a while, and like any other preparation without vinegar or preservatives will go mouldy. They are fine for up to three months, but are so good that I doubt that you will keep them for so long.

They go well with mozzarella, prosciutto, cheese, boiled meats and bread.

Melanzane alla Parmigiana alla Moda di Anna
Anna's Eggplant Parmigiana

Not the traditional, layered, oven-baked dish of eggplant (aubergine) but individually dressed and baked slices. They are a very good antipasto *and go well into a sandwich. I have yet to make them as well as Anna, my mother-in-law, but my adaptation is good enough. This deceptively simple-looking dish is full of traps.*

Serves as many as you like
PREPARATION TIME: 30 MINUTES
COOKING TIME: 6 MINUTES

slices of eggplant (aubergine) from firm
and ripe fruit, not quite 1 cm (½ in) thick

olive oil for frying

salt

parmesan cheese, grated

a leaf of basil per slice of eggplant (aubergine)

shredded mozzarella

TOMATO SAUCE
4 tablespoons olive oil
2 cloves garlic, whole
1 x 400 g (14 oz) can Roma tomatoes

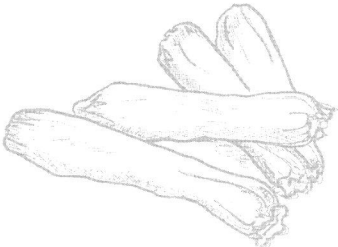

Fry the eggplant slices in plenty of oil till they brown. Drain on paper towels.

To make the tomato sauce, heat a skillet, add the oil (which should be hot almost immediately) and fry the garlic. Remove and discard the garlic. Add the tomatoes after crushing them with a fork and cook for 20 minutes. This will make enough sauce for at least 30 slices.

Preheat the oven to 180°C (350°F).

Place the eggplant slices on a baking dish, preferably a flat one without high sides. Sprinkle some salt and parmesan cheese on each slice. Place a leaf of basil on each as well. Cover the basil with shredded mozzarella, but not too much as it will flood the slice and harden into a pool of cheese. (Resist the temptation to use bocconcini: they don't melt evenly and have little flavour.)

Top with some tomato sauce; not too much or the slice will be wet. The perfection of this dish is achieved by the fine-tuning of all the parts.

Bake for 6 minutes or until the mozzarella has a tinge of brown. Tilt the baking tray on one side to remove any oil that has oozed out during the cooking.

Serve hot or cold. With bread and salad, you almost have a meal. We enjoy this dish for lunch when we are out on the block, picking apples, sultana grapes or oranges.

Baccalà Mantecato
Creamed Cod

Baccalà is made from those wonderful-looking dry fish hanging — less and less frequently — in continental delis. It is cod fished in the northern Atlantic Ocean and traditionally wind-dried. The Italians made vast use of it through the centuries as did the French, the Spaniards and the Portuguese.

There is something odd about a fish from the waters below the Arctic Circle becoming a perfect partner for olives, olive oil and tomatoes, and yet this is one of the best gastronomic partnerships ever. Salt was a precious commodity in the northern European countries which is why, I presume, cod was wind-dried. I am also sure that cod was exchanged for salt and many other commodities. The Venetians certainly had a big trade going on with the colder countries.

The problem with baccalà is that it takes several days to reconstitute in fresh, preferably running, water. Another problem is that the quality of baccalà available in Australia is not, in my experience, the best, which is why many of us have opted for salted fillets of fish instead. These fillets are not as refined as the real thing, but acceptable. You need to soak them for several days with many changes of water before use.

One of the uses in the kitchen for salted fillets is for a dish called baccalà mantecato, *creamed baccalà. The French call it* brandade de morue, *and some smart chefs serve it under that name in Australia. The Italian restaurants, by and large, ignore baccalà as they have consistently ignored the more challenging dishes of the Italian tradition. The best I have had, and it was real baccalà, was at a restaurant in Adelaide called Chianti.*

The mantecato *is one thing that makes Italian food writers go completely silly. They begin talking of the white froth, the ethereal cream, the white cloud of ecstasy and so on in over-the-top fashion.*

It is really that good? Try it for yourself with this very simple recipe and decide.

Serves 8 as an antipasto

SOAKING TIME: 2 DAYS
PREPARATION TIME: 45 MINUTES

1 kg (2 lb) salted cod

1 L (4 cups) milk

2 L (8 cups) water

5 peppercorns

2 bay leaves

1 clove garlic, finely chopped

250 mL (1 cup) flavoursome but light olive oil

1 medium-sized potato, boiled, peeled
and chopped roughly

a few drops of lemon juice

1–2 tablespoons chilled water

a pinch of freshly ground black pepper

a pinch of chopped parsley

After soaking in frequently refreshed water for 2 days, place the cod in a pot with the milk, water, peppercorns and bay leaves and gently bring to the boil. Simmer for a few minutes and remove from the heat. Let the cod cool to the point where you can handle the flesh. Remove bones, skin and other hard bits, especially towards the tail end.

Place the flaked fish in a food processor with the garlic. Give it a few quick turns to break it down and begin to add the oil as if doing a mayonnaise. Add the potato and incorporate it well with a few more turns. Keep going with the oil and a few drops of lemon juice until you have a mixture of soft consistency. Taste to be sure that all the elements have come together well. If you feel there is enough oil do not add more: you may not have to use the whole cup. At this final stage add the chilled water; the water will emulsify the oil and make the mixture look lighter in colour.

Place in a container, sprinkle with a little fresh black pepper and parsley.

Serve with slices of grilled yellow polenta, drizzled with more oil if you wish. I find the contrast between cold cod and hot polenta very appealing. The polenta can also be served runny if it is beautifully made.

Another embellishment, although not a necessary one, is the addition of tiny Sicilian capers, the ones that you can buy in specialist shops. These come salted. Wash the sea salt away and soak in water. Change the water a few times, dry well on a tea towel (this may take several hours) and place in a jar. Top with olive oil. They are indispensable for recipes like *vitello tonnato*, baked fish or smoked salmon salad.

Note: Also see the recipe for Baccalà in Two Ways in Piatti Forti (see page 172).

POLLO IN BIANCO ALLA MANIERA CINESE
STEEPED CHICKEN IN THE CHINESE MANNER

This is a Chinese preparation known as white chicken. Cheong Liew has a recipe for it in his book
My Food and Stephanie Alexander has a recipe — it is rather a method — in The Cook's Companion.
Tony Tan has also had it published as Hainanese Chicken on several occasions.

Why give it here, in a book of Italian recipes? If you are as crazy for chicken as I am, you need no explanation!
This makes a fantastic antipasto anytime, anywhere, but especially during the warmer months. It is elegant, satisfying
as a method, and a vast improvement on the old boiled chook Italian mothers used to serve with giardiniera.
When I tasted it for the first time I thought I was in heaven.

Serves 6 or more
PREPARATION TIME: 45 MINUTES
1 knob ginger, halved
2 spring onions (scallions)
1 × 1.7 kg (3 ½ lb) free-range chicken
cold water
ice

Bring a pot of water to the boil. Place the ginger and spring onions in the cavity of the chicken. Immerse the chicken in the boiling water and leave for 1–2 minutes. You will be amazed to see what impurities are left behind! At this point I have learnt from Cheong Liew to chill the chicken in very cold water and ice. It seems to set the skin, which you must not bruise or break at any point. Use an old cloth to ease the bird in and out of the pot.

In the meantime bring a second pot of water to the boil and immerse the chicken for 1 minute. Remove the chicken to allow the water to boil again. Repeat this operation a couple of times. By now the chicken should be fairly hot. Immerse the chicken in the water for the final time and turn off the flame or remove the pot from the stove. Cover with aluminium foil and a lid and leave for about 35 minutes, after which the chicken should be cooked. Check under the thighs and do not panic if there is a slight tinge of pink.

This chicken should not be overcooked. In the end only practice will refine your ability to cook this dish to perfection. Most people will tell you to let the chicken cool naturally. This is wrong and if you do that, the bird will continue to cook and turn grey. Therefore I encourage you to place it in chilled water.

The aroma of ginger and spring onions makes this an addictive dish. When you finally slice it for serving you will notice a layer of jelly between the skin. The flesh will be firm and white, with a texture that no other method of cooking will deliver.

Serve with Peperoncini Ripieni di Capperi e Acciughe (see page 33) for an Italian conclusion or in the Chinese manner, with a dipping sauce of pounded spring onions, ginger, garlic and salt-reduced soy. Either way strips of cucumber and crunchy lettuce could accompany.

LINGUA DI BUE LESSA
POACHED OX TONGUE

Not for everyone, but a classic nonetheless. Buy tongues in brine from your local butcher.

Serves 6 or more
PREPARATION TIME: 5 MINUTES
COOKING TIME: SEVERAL HOURS
OF SLOW BOILING

1 ox tongue

4 L (3 quarts) water

1 whole carrot

1 whole stick celery

1 whole onion

1 tablespoon ground allspice

Place all ingredients in a pot and simmer. The ox tongue will need about 3 hours. Feel it with your fingers — when it is ready, it is not springy any more.

Remove the membrane that encases the meat.

Slice the tongue at an angle and serve with anything you like: a salad; salsa verde and boiled waxy potatoes; hoisin sauce; coat the sliced tongue in egg and fry again; or grill or cut into julienne strips and serve with olives or *giardiniera*.

PORK, PORK, AND MORE PORK

Like many Italians from all over the world I too have kept a pig in the backyard. Ours was always called Maurice, year after year. Each Maurice was sacrificed on the altar of necessity with a ritual that took place in January when the cold was most intense. Santolo Severino Battistella — *santolo* is the word for Godfather — was the high priest of this sacrifice: he was tall, he had a grey moustache, travelled on a shiny black bike and wrapped himself in a black cloak. He also had a wide-brimmed hat and a bag full of scary knives. He used to arrive fairly early and make a grand entrance into the yard. You could hear his voice barking out orders right, left and centre and superfluous comments like: 'You bloody de Pieri women, you never have enough hot water ready — have you run out of wood, you fools?' Thereupon my mother, who was never short of a quip and who resented being lumped with the de Pieris — like all Italian women she kept her maiden name — would reply in a less than complimentary way, setting herself on a collision course with my father, whose mother had been a Battistella.

Santolo wanted hot water to shave the pig after he had killed it. He needed lots of it to pour over the pig's skin to remove every bristle or any dirt. There were three 44-gallon half-drums of water with fires going under them, and yet there was never enough water for Santolo Severino. I think that speaks volumes about the importance of hygiene when dealing with pigs. (I cannot say that Aussie pork is treated with the same respect. The burning or other general mutilation of the trotters and the cheeks does not amount to good hygienic practice when the scum is still left on the skin.)

I ran away on each occasion the pig had to be killed. I plugged my ears with my fingers to block out Maurice's screams; he not only understood his fate the moment the five men walked into his pen, placed a noose around his snout and grabbed him by the tail, but would also scream and whine as the men dispatched his soul.

The blood was always collected and was made into a delectable dessert called *baldon*, a confection with sugar, orange peel and sultanas.

After the shaving Maurice was hoisted by the back legs and split into two halves. I will never forget the sight of steaming guts pouring out into the gutter and the annual truce between the cats and the dog.

The liver, heart and kidneys were eaten first. The bladder was cleaned and later would become the container for rendered fat.

That was the end of procedures for the day; Santolo would return a day later to make the salami. I was too little to be allowed to mix with the adults, who were busy at work. One year they got rid of me by sending me on an errand. I was to go to a particular neighbour and collect a salami mould. He understood at once the nature of my errand, and promptly attached a rope to the discarded axle of an old cart. A heavy piece of equipment, as I recall. When I quizzed the bloke — for I wasn't 100 per cent stupid — he very persuasively told me that the salami meat would be forced through the holes in the axle and into the appropriate casings — thus the salami mould.

I believed him and proceeded to drag this metal bar through the snow for a good 3 kilometres. When I finally made it home, exhausted and wet, the salami-making was over and done with. Everyone laughed at me while they were washing their greasy hands. It was an important lesson, perhaps one not acceptable these days, but one that served me well later in life. Here, I will let you in on some tricks so that you too can enjoy some preserved pork.

La Pancetta alla Casalinga
PORK BELLY IN THE COUNTRY STYLE

Pork belly is exciting in any language: ask the Chinese who treat it reverentially.

Serves many

PREPARATION TIME: 10 MINUTES,
THEN 2 MINUTES PER DAY FOR THREE DAYS

5 kg (10 lb) pork belly, cut into two pieces,
ribs removed

salt

fine black pepper

hot chilli powder (optional)

Remove the skins from the belly (the skins can be used in many ways — see opposite page, for example). Place the belly meat on a stainless-steel tray and cover with fine salt on all sides. Make sure the tray is inclined so that the water drawn out by the salt runs off the tray and into another. If you are doing this at home you can safely carry out this procedure in your garage if you live in a cold climate and operate in the winter months, whereas those who live in warm climates can do it in the fridge.

For 3 days make sure the meat remains covered in salt — the same salt — if it slides off the meat, push it back on. On the fourth day wash the meat under a running tap and dry it with a clean cloth. Sprinkle very, very liberally with fine black pepper or hot chilli powder and hang somewhere cold and ventilated for at least 3 weeks.

You will find this pancetta delectable if you cut it thinly; it may taste salty otherwise. This is great as a base for matriciana sauce, to stuff into quails or to flavour roast chicken and so on.

If you want a more sophisticated-looking product, one that remains rosy and fresh inside, once it has undergone the procedure outlined above, roll the belly on itself as tightly as you can and tie it with string like a *salame*. Wrap in wax paper and tie again, taking care to close both ends. The paper is not as good as the gut casing that is traditionally used, but it will do the job. The pancetta in this case will take longer to cure — 3 months in a cool place — because it is rolled.

Cotica della Pancetta
BELLY SKINS

If you think I am fanatical about pork, let me tell you that I am justified: Italian cuisine would not waste one iota of this precious animal and in doing so it has invented the most tasty dishes. So if you want to know the secrets of Italian cooking, you have to put up with this information.

This is a great dish if you like pork and one of the few recipes that employ a sweet ingredient. You can also omit the sweet sultanas and place the roll in a pot with tomatoes for a spaghetti sauce that will have all the hallmarks of authenticity.

Serves 4

PREPARATION TIME: 10 MINUTES

COOKING TIME: ABOUT 2 HOURS
OF SLOW COOKING

2 pieces pork skins, each measuring
20 cm x 10 cm (8 in x 4 in)

2 cloves garlic, chopped

2 tablespoons sultanas

2 tablespoons grated parmesan cheese

2 tablespoons freshly chopped Italian
(flat-leaf) parsley

olive oil

salt and freshly ground black pepper

Make sure that you have washed and scrubbed the skins: no hairy bits please — burn them off if you have to — and scrub a bit more if unsure.

Lay the skins on a bench with the inside facing up. Distribute the garlic, sultanas, parmesan cheese and parsley evenly, roll up and tie with strong kitchen string.

Place in a heavy casserole dish with a little olive oil, season with salt and pepper, and cook gently, adding a little water now and then if the rolls stick too severely to the pot. Cook with the lid on until tender and the skin melts in the mouth.

Serve with grilled polenta.

PESCE IN CARPIONE
FRIED FISH PRESERVED IN VINEGAR

Carpione is not a big carp, but refers to a method of preparing fish for a colourful and tasty antipasto. When the lakes and rivers of northern Italy were clean and had plenty of fish such as pike and eel, this method was very popular. The dish is similar to the Venetian in saor (white vinegar) method, but the inclusion of carrots makes it rather sweet. It looks very pretty and tastes very gusty.

As pikes and eels are not easily available, mackerel is a fine substitute. Indeed, the so-called Indian mackerel, when fresh and moist, is great in this dish.

Serves 10
PREPARATION TIME: 1 HOUR

6 fresh mackerels, gutted and ready for deep-frying

plain (all-purpose) flour

oil for frying

2 carrots, peeled and sliced in rounds 2 mm (¼ in) thick

1 cup diced onions

1 cup diced celery

a few whole peppercorns

500 mL (2 cups) chicken stock

250 mL (1 cup) white vinegar

4 fresh bay leaves

Roll the fish in flour and deep-fry.

Place carrots, onions, celery, peppercorns and stock in a casserole and cook with the lid on until the carrots are soft. Remove from the stove and add the white vinegar.

In the meantime remove all the bones, the head and other unpleasant bits from the fish. Keep some skin on.

Place the filleted fish in a ceramic bowl, scatter the bay leaves over the fish and cover with the cooled carrots and vinegar dressing. Refrigerate for several hours before serving. The fish will keep in the refrigerator for days.

SARDELE IN SAOR
SARDINES PRESERVED IN WHITE VINEGAR

A dish similar to fried fish preserved in vinegar (see previous page), but its character comes from the sardines and the sultanas. This dish keeps for up to 5 days if properly refrigerated.

Serves 6

PREPARATION TIME: 20 MINUTES
AND MACERATION TIME OVERNIGHT

plain (all-purpose) flour to coat the sardines
18 fresh sardines, gutted and heads removed
olive oil for frying
3 onions, thinly sliced
125 mL (½ cup) white vinegar
3 whole bay leaves
10 whole peppercorns
½ cup sultanas
salt

Lightly flour the sardines and fry in just enough oil. Remove the fish and, with the oil still hot, add the onions and fry until golden and soft. Add the vinegar. Cook a little to concentrate.

Lay the sardines in a ceramic bowl, sprinkle with the bay leaves, peppercorns, sultanas and salt, and pour over the onion mixture. Rest in the refrigerator for a day before serving. Will keep and improve for a week.

THE MAIZE CYCLE

Polenta (cornmeal) is ground maize, and has a long and controversial pedigree. It was the food of the poor, the cause of an infamous vitamin deficiency called pelagra which could, in turn, cause madness. It is also one food that means a lot to me.

My parents grew maize like all other northern Italian farmers; sowed, thinned and fertilised it by hand. The top leaves were cut off in midsummer, two notches above the cobs, to let the sun in to ripen the cobs, which, when ripe, were picked by hand. We also stripped the dried leaves for fodder for the cows and then cut the stalks into lengths which were fed to the cows as a kind of after-dinner mint. One of my jobs was to retrieve the pieces that had not been eaten from the manger and chop them up into bedding for the cows. When the bedding was soiled, it was removed and taken to the pile of manure which was our organic fertiliser. The leaves around the cob that were clean and in good condition were dried and used to stuff mattresses.

Maize, as you can gather, was of critical importance to humans and animals, a tremendous resource where a family had to support itself on a few acres. This strict economy is a far cry from the experiences of Australian farmers who, with plenty of land, and often with water resources nearby, do not even bother to grow a carrot. I cannot comprehend how these people expect to live well in a physical and spiritual sense without growing any vegetables or making their own bread.

We had a special machine to strip the kernels from the cobs but it could not possibly strip each single one. Good housekeeping dictated that the brown cores be strewn around the section of the yard where the poultry was kept so they could peck at what was left. Once the chooks had given them a good going over they became both kindling and fuel or, for us reckless kids, an alternative to the shiny paper of the weekly, Vatican-sponsored *Famiglia Cristiana* magazine, a Veneto equivalent of the telephone book on a hook in the old-fashioned outdoor Aussie dunnies. Recycling ahead of its time.

My mother made polenta almost every day for more than half a century. It is cooked in a special pot that sits in the stove or hangs from a chain over the flames, with water and salt, sometimes enriched by cheese, butter or other types of fat. Generally, making polenta was a long affair but a simple one as long as one condition was observed: there were to be no lumps. I can still hear my father once saying that he had found lumps and the mortified look on my mother's face. Nothing could be more humiliating for a respectable housewife than producing a polenta with lumps. If lumps did form in her polenta, it was because she was distracted by the fire — or the lack of it, to be more precise — which was fuelled by dried maize cobs.

In other books other writers have alluded to polenta: Stefano Manfredi, for example, explains how his father had a big say in how the polenta-making ritual brought his family together. Australian chefs have demonstrated considerable skill with polenta: they have invented creative, spunky dishes featuring polenta, taking advantage of its colour or its texture.

The polenta available in Australia is very good, especially if mixed with a little semolina, which gives the final product a softer, less grainy feel. In the old days polenta used to take a long time to finish cooking because the flour was of poor quality. Not that the original fruit wasn't any good — it possibly was — but the maize was harvested in October and kept until the following summer, usually on the floor of a granary; those kernels couldn't have tasted all that good being there all that time and possibly with mice running through the cobs!

If old-style polenta takes a long time to cook, by contrast Australian polenta is a model of efficiency. Use a bit of common-sense and you will succeed.

La Polenta

POLENTA

Serves 10

COOKING TIME: 20 MINUTES

2 L (8 cups) hot water

salt

3 cups polenta (cornmeal)

Gradually add the polenta to the lightly salted hot water by allowing it to fall from your hand from above the pot like sand through your fingers. If the water is *not* boiling, you will be able to stir in all the polenta without lumps forming. As the temperature rises, the flour will intregrate with the water and thicken. Stir all the time, and if you have used too much of the flour and the mixture is too thick, add a little water. I taste for salt and perhaps add some parmesan cheese. When the polenta is smooth and does not taste of raw maize, it is ready.

You can use this sloppy polenta with anything that has been braising for a while: chicken, beef and fish stews, vegetables and mushrooms, grilled sausages, quails, liver cooked with onions and so on.

Alternatively, pour the polenta into a flat baking dish where it will cool and become firm. At that point it can be grilled or oven baked for 20 minutes.

As a grilled slice polenta will accompany many creative Australian dishes — as a base for fried eggplant (aubergine) slices, goat's cheese, rocket (arugula), artichokes, prosciutto and so on. For me grilled polenta is good with either baked or fried fish, *baccalà mantecato* and lumps of parmesan cheese.

Baked polenta can be dressed with cheese, roasted capsicums and fine *salame* or pancetta.

After you have poured the hot polenta into a tray some will remain stuck to the sides of the pot. Let it dry, even for a day, and peel these skins off. They are delicious with parmesan cheese.

Veneto Salame on Hot Polenta (see page 54)

VENETO SALAME ON HOT POLENTA

Like many other dishes, this is one that can be breakfast, antipasto, *a snack or an addition to a simple dinner.*

In a good delicatessen find a good Veneto *salame* like the *soppressa*, which contains a higher proportion of fat.

Prepare a quantity of polenta following the recipe on page 52 and pour into a flat tray to let it set. When cold and firm, cut the necessary number of slices or squares, place on a heavy-based baking tray and place in a hot oven.

When the polenta is hot and crisp, remove from the oven and arrange thinly sliced *salame* over the squares. The polenta must be hot enough to warm up the *salame*, and the meat slices thin enough almost to melt.

Resist any temptation to embellish. Replace *salame* with cheese if vegetarian.

TORTINO DI POLENTA CON CIPOLLA IN UMIDO
POLENTA TART SMOTHERED WITH ONIONS

Serves 10

PREPARATION TIME: 2 HOURS

1 quantity cooked polenta

4 eggs

2 cups grated parmesan cheese

10 small onions, sliced

2 tablespoons butter

olive oil

3 cloves garlic, chopped

2 whole salted sardine fillets

Make polenta according to the recipe on page 52 — enough to fill a 23cm (9 inch) tart ring — and let it cool completely. Pass it through a mouli and incorporate the eggs and parmesan cheese or some other cheese which will melt into the polenta.

Preheat the oven to 180°C (350°F)

Place the mixture into the tart ring and bake until a brown skin forms on top. This tortino will rise in the oven and will, naturally, fall as it cools.

Braise the onions slowly with the garlic and sardines in butter and olive oil until soft. Cook for 1 ½ hours for desired effect.

To serve, slice a piece of tortino and place some onions over it.

Tortino di Verdure Cotte
Braised Vegetable Pie

*Italians love all sorts of greens, especially those like broccoli, silverbeet and spinach which can be first cooked
in boiling water until soft and then braised with onions, garlic and chilli with oil or butter. The best greens
in this category are usually from the wild — in the north of Italy the best and the sweetest were the plants of
red poppies before they flower. Curly endive is quite good. Chinese broccoli (choy sum),
hard stalks removed, are absolutely stunning and readily available.
The pie pastry must be thin. Therein lies the elegance of this dish, even though it is drawn from rustic cuisine.*

Serves 10

PREPARATION TIME: 10 MINUTES FOR THE
PASTRY; 20 MINUTES FOR THE VEGETABLES

COOKING TIME: 10 MINUTES

PASTRY (FOR TWO TORTINI)

3 cups plain (all-purpose) flour

a pinch of bicarbonate of soda (baking soda)

3 eggs

4 tablespoons ghee (clarified butter)
or lard, warmed

hot water

FILLING

6 bunches Chinese broccoli

4 tablespoons olive oil

3 cloves garlic, chopped

1 onion, finely chopped

1 pinch minced chilli (optional)

some whole slices of pancetta

salt

1/2 cup grated parmesan cheese

1 egg yolk

To make the pastry, sift the flour with the bicarbonate of soda. Make a well and incorporate the eggs and the warm ghee. Add enough hot water to combine into smooth dough. Do not overwork. This dough should be quite soft but not sticky.

Wash and trim the Chinese broccoli and cook in plenty of boiling water until soft. Cool and chop.

Heat the oil, add the garlic, onion, chilli, pancetta, and broccoli and cook until the flavours have amalgamated and the residual water has evaporated. This is very important. Remove the pancetta and discard. Taste for salt. Let the mixture cool.

Preheat the oven to 180°C (350°F).

On a floured surface roll out the pastry to 2 mm (1/4 inch) thickness. Line a flat 23cm (9 inch) tart ring right up to the sides. Fill the pie with the cooled, cooked broccoli and sprinkle generously with parmesan cheese. Roll out another thin sheet of pastry and lay it over the top and over the edge. Cut off excess pastry and press the edges together with your fingers. Baste with egg yolk and cook until golden, about 10 minutes.

This tortino is eaten by itself, hot or cold. It is a stupendous first course. With the omission of the pancetta it makes a vegetarian dish. Cold, it makes a perfect addition to your picnic basket or *antipasto* platter.

BRODO, ZUPPE E MINESTRE
BROTHS, SOUPS AND MINESTRONE

Soups can be made with anything, be thick or thin, with or without pasta or rice. The panorama of Italian food in this respect is as open as the range of *antipasto*. Minestrone is about all we used to get in Australian–Italian restaurants; badly made minestrone, with everything in it, especially tomato paste and soft pasta that has been sitting for hours, if not days. If restaurants have been setting the pace in terms of what people eat at home or try to follow the same trend, then they are, by and large, guilty of not exposing diners to the wholesome, voluptuous world of Italian soups.

In trying to open up this world of possibilities I have selected the ideas I like: some are old, some new, but all are possible, even those that seem a little fancy.

I am a firm believer that a good soup usually requires a good stock, though some recipes here only use water. Stock comes up constantly in the section on risotto so at this point it is important to clarify what I mean by a stock. What all mammas use regularly is chicken stock without which there isn't going to be a good flavouring agent for risotto or soups. Once again, many versions exist, all of which no doubt satisfy their advocates. A good stock should be simmered rather than boiled. I usually

Zuppa di Pane o della Felicità (page 63)

do not add vegetables because when the stock is used more often than not I will combine it with many vegetables, in minestrone, for instance.

Generally I simply use a good boiler or two, cooked for a couple of hours at a simmer with the addition of celery and onions towards the end to try to preserve some fresh aromas. My mother used to put carrots, onions, celery and even the odd tomato from the start, as most Italian mammas do. I agree with the practice of plunging the bird/s into a bath of hot water before adding them to the stockpot. You will be amazed to see how much debris is left behind. For the rest, it is all simple as long as whatever you are cooking is always submerged in liquid and you skim and clean the stock as you go.

I also know for a fact that in Italy people add stock cubes to their stocks because that provides an element of 'kick' otherwise known as salt. Beware, however, of stock cubes with MSG. There is also a huge difference between a good-quality stock cube and what we know commercially as chicken booster. Lines must be drawn!

For a beef stock, which is good mixed with chicken for a dish of tortellini, use cheap cuts of meat and start the stock with hot water after blanching. Those rich and concentrated stocks that seem to find their way into everything are another matter altogether. There are plenty of instructions for demi-glace, as it is known, in other books. There is a place for this type of stock in the restaurant kitchen, even in Italian cooking. It provides a sauce to accompany meats of all kinds and loves to be soaked up with bread. The so-called Brit-pack boys, the new chefs out of England, have no hesitation putting demi-glace over fish, and I think it is terrific, especially with Murray cod. This sauce takes a long time to prepare and Italian mammas certainly never used it, relying chiefly on the self-saucing quality of their dishes, back when a little oil or fat was not regarded as a health hazard.

Cooks who undertake the long preparation of this sauce know the value of skimming the stock while the beef and veal bones are slowly ticking away on simmer, as they know that fat boiling into the stock will ruin it. I'll give you a tip that I have not read in any books so far: when your stock is hot and the bones are releasing residual fat, plunge a lot of ice into the pot — it will bring more muck to the surface and reduce that tedious task of skimming the stock. This is a good trick especially if you are planning to let the pot simmer overnight.

ZUPPA DI LENTICCHE CON PASTA A TUBETTI

SHORT PASTA TUBES WITH LENTILS

I love serving this soup to vegetarian friends and it is a Sunday special in our family.
Commercial short pasta tubes do not contain egg. The vegetarian content is guaranteed.

Serves 6

PREPARATION AND COOKING TIME: 1 ½
HOURS, MOSTLY TIME TO COOK THE LENTILS

500 g (1 lb) lentils
3 cloves garlic, crushed

salt

olive oil

1 x 400 g (14 oz) can Italian peeled tomatoes,
chopped (or fresh tomatoes, peeled and
chopped)

a pinch of sugar

300 g (10 oz) short pasta

parmesan cheese, grated

fresh herbs

chilli

extra dash of olive oil

Rinse lentils and remove impurities. Soak in water for 30 minutes. Place lentils with garlic in a medium-sized pot and cover generously with water. Place on moderate heat and cook until soft and most of the water has evaporated. Add a pinch of salt as you go and make sure the water does not evaporate too quickly.

In the meantime, heat a little oil in a saucepan and add the tomatoes; reduce to a pulp. Add a pinch of salt and cook until a simple tomato sauce is ready. Given the poor quality of tomatoes — including imported ones — you may add a touch of sugar.

Now you have cooked lentils and tomato sauce. Cook the pasta in salted water — if not using short tubes, then broken spaghetti. Drain when cooked *al dente* and keep some cooking liquid. Combine the pasta and the lentils, add tomato sauce to your liking and parmesan cheese, herbs, chilli and oil. The soup should be thickish.

It is also delicious with a few leaves of rocket (arugula) and, if you wish, swirl through a teaspoon of balsamic vinegar.

PASTA E FAGIOLI

Or pasta with beans to you, as John McGrath of the Adelaide Review once put it. Pasta e fagioli is not just a soup. This initially unappealing-looking brown concoction epitomises the essence of northern Italian, and particularly Veneto, cooking. A study of its parts is a foray into anthropology or any of the sciences that study people, their culture and their environment. These things have to be said because there is very little point presenting this soup — as many other books do — without the right context. I cannot imagine why an unaware reader should get excited about this soup without any supporting explanation.

After the discovery of America, maize was introduced to Europe. The Veneto peasants made it an important crop, chiefly for polenta and animal fodder. In subsistence farming every opportunity had to be exploited to the utmost degree. Hence beans were planted with the maize. On average, it was one bean plant to every sixth cornstalk so the bean plant was supported as it grew. After the maize cobs were harvested, the farmer would return to collect baskets upon baskets of beans, usually borlotti. They were dried in their pods, which were spread on every bit of pavement in the yard to absorb the autumn sun and then stored for the winter.

During the miserably cold winter months the fagioli pot would bubble on the hot surface of the cucina economica almost every day. In January, after the slaughter of the pig, various bits of pork — all the bones, trotters, ears and cheeks — would find their way into the soup. The bones flavoured the soup and the bits of meat provided extra protein, or at least the illusion of having eaten meat with one's meal.

Pasta e fagioli can be prepared ahead, even a couple of days, and it improves on keeping.

Serves 8 or more

PREPARATION TIME: 10 MINUTES
COOKING TIME: 3 HOURS

500 g (1 lb) borlotti beans
soaked for a few hours

3 tablespoons tomato paste

8 medium-sized potatoes,
peeled and roughly cut

2 cloves garlic, crushed

2 medium-sized carrots, cut into a few pieces

2 onions, whole

2 stalks celery, cut into a few pieces

1 small chilli (optional)

salt

5 L (4 quarts) water

300 g (10 oz) thin egg fettuccine

parmesan cheese, grated

olive oil

red-wine vinegar

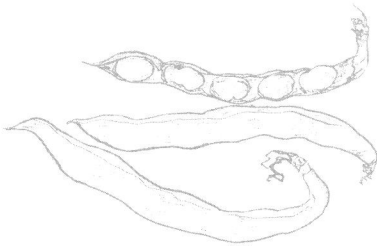

Place all the ingredients except the fettuccine, parmesan cheese, oil and vinegar in a large pot and cover with cold water. Boil for 3 or even 4 hours, making sure that nothing sticks to the bottom of the pot. Water will evaporate, beans will expand and some will burst, potatoes will break down and the vegetables will soften. The whole mixture will have the colour of a strong *caffè latte*. At this point let it cool.

As soon as you can work without burning yourself, remove the vegetables, including any potato that is intact, and at least half of the beans. Pass all this through the mouli or press it through a sieve or somehow pulp it.

Put everything back in the pot: you should now have a brown, soft concoction that is not too firm and not too watery, with half of the beans still intact. This is your base. Now bring it gently to the boil, add some water if it's too thick and drop in the fettuccine. The pasta starch will amalgamate beautifully with the soup. Again, be careful not to catch the bottom of the pot.

When the pasta is cooked, stir in the parmesan cheese.

At the table each diner should have access to a little olive oil and vinegar, preferably red. A tablespoon of oil and vinegar tickles the nostrils and adds two extra flavour dimensions that I promise will please and surprise.

The soup base can be stored in the refrigerator and will improve. When needed pull some out and proceed as above. *Pasta e fagioli* is no longer considered a peasant dish. The addition of good olive oil and fine cheese, two critical flavours, place it in another dimension. It is now in every cookery book — one by Claudia Roden comes to mind — and it has been adopted as a nostalgia dish. At Harry's Dolci, on the Giudecca side of Venice, a favourite outdoor dining venue on the Feast of the Redeemer, when amazing fireworks are exploded in the midnight sky, *pasta e fagioli* is served at around 2 a.m. immediately followed by crispy fresh watermelon.

ZUPPA DI RISO E VERZA
SAVOY CABBAGE AND RICE SOUP

A dish best enjoyed on a cold winter's day. Savoy cabbage is the wrinkly variety, which is softer and smaller than the compact one.

Serves 6
PREPARATION TIME: 30–40 MINUTES

1 onion, chopped
80 mL (⅓ cup) good olive oil
2 cups diced potato
1 Savoy cabbage, shredded
1 cup diced fresh tomato
2–3 L (1 ½–2 ½ quarts) chicken stock
2 cups rice
salt and pepper
1 cup pecorino chunks

Sauté the onion in the olive oil until translucent. Add the potato, cabbage and tomato. If the pot is too small add the cabbage gradually — it will soon reduce.

When the cabbage is soft, add all the stock at once, and cook until the potatoes are soft. Add the rice, making sure that it will not absorb all the stock. If it does, add more stock. Stir from time to time. Season with salt and pepper. The rice should be cooked until soft. The soup should be creamy and runny after the addition of big chunks of pecorino cheese.

Zuppa di Pane o della Felicità
SOUP OF HAPPINESS

My brother Sergio named this the 'soup of happiness' because the large amount of fibre in it is supposed to help digestion and act as a body cleanser. Sometime after the soup you are supposed to feel light and therefore happy.

Robyn Dixon, a friend who has been for some years the Age newspaper's Moscow correspondent, was on her way to Russia when she stopped to visit us in Treviso for a home-cooked Italian meal before the uncertainties of the cuisine that lay ahead. Her visit coincided with the visit of Steve Letts, an ABC old-timer. My brother was concocting such soup and looked more like a possessed alchemist than a cook. I was rather embarrassed that he would actually dish this up to guests who are, as they say in Italian, buone forchette, good forks. I had nothing to fear because the soup went down well — if you forgive the expression — and to this day we laugh about the concept of happiness achieved intestinally. The soup became, in our circle of friends, quite a legend.

Serves 6–8
PREPARATION TIME: 10 MINUTES
COOKING TIME: 30–40 MINUTES

2–3 cups diced vegetables, for example, carrots, celery, onions

olive oil

4 ripe Roma (plum) tomatoes, skinned and seeded

500 g (1 lb) stale, good crusty bread (not sourdough), broken into pieces

3–4 L (2 ½–3 quarts) chicken stock or water

basil leaves

parmesan cheese

extra-virgin olive oil

Gently fry the vegetables in a bit of oil. Add the tomatoes. Add the bread and the stock, a little at a time, until you see that the bread cannot soak it up any more. A little milk may give some creaminess. Add the basil and parmesan cheese, and let your guests decide if they want any extra-virgin olive oil.

Pasta e Piselli

Pasta and Peas

This dish is a vegetarian triumph. Strict ones can omit the cheese and add some extra-virgin olive oil instead.

Serves 6–8

PREPARATION TIME: 10 MINUTES
COOKING TIME: 40 MINUTES OR LESS

300 mL (1 1/5 cups) Tomato Sauce (see page 37)

3 large potatoes (I prefer to use old ones), diced

400 g (13 oz) peas (shelled weight)

salt

300 g (10 oz) short pasta or more

grated parmesan cheese

freshly ground pepper

fresh herbs, for example, basil or mint

Cook tomato sauce with potatoes until the potatoes are soft. To achieve this you have to add water and stir at regular intervals to make sure nothing sticks to the bottom of the pot. Cook with the lid on to minimise evaporation. When the potatoes are ready, add the peas — from a can if you want — and adjust salt.

Cook the pasta until *al dente*, then combine with tomato sauce and peas. Add parmesan cheese, pepper and herbs to taste. You should be able to taste the pasta and the peas quite separately.

Minestrone di Campagna

Country-Style Minestrone

Serves 6–8

PREPARATION TIME: 30 MINUTES
COOKING TIME: 30–40 MINUTES

extra-virgin olive oil

1 cup chopped onions

2 cloves garlic

3 potatoes, diced

2 cups peeled and chopped fresh tomatoes

salt

3 cups chopped zucchini (courgette)

2 cups diced string beans, blanched

extra olive oil

parmesan cheese, grated

Heat oil in a deep saucepan and cook the onions and garlic until translucent. Add the potatoes and tomatoes and cook until fairly soft. Add a good pinch of salt and enough water to cover. Salt is a personal choice, but where potatoes are involved you really need it. Water will help to break down the potatoes. (If you like, replace the water with chicken stock.)

Add zucchini, soften quite a lot and finally, add the beans. Add more water if needed.

This is a rough and ready soup. Finish it with olive oil and parmesan cheese.

ZUPPA DI PESCE PASTA E FAGIOLI
FISH AND HOME-MADE PASTA SOUP WITH BEANS

I find this dish appealing because it combines the earthy flavours of beans with the taste of seafood.
This is also a quirky dish because it introduces the softness of home-made pasta to balance the crunch of the beans.
It goes without saying that the better the seafood, the better the final result.

Beware of tough cannellini beans. I hate them when they need to be cooked for a fortnight. Make sure you buy them
from a reputable supplier. The alternative is to use chickpeas — remove the skins by rubbing them together when
they are still in the soaking water — or, the best option, some fresh borlotti.

Serves 6

COOKING TIME: 2 HOURS TO PRE-COOK
THE BEANS, BUT DURING THIS TIME
YOU MAKE THE PASTA AND STOCK

300 g (10 oz) cannellini beans or other beans

2 potatoes

200 g (7 oz) home-made pasta,
roughly cut (see page 97)

2 crabs cut into quarters

500 g (1 lb) white fish fillets

12 uncooked prawns

24 uncooked clams

24 uncooked mussels

chopped Italian (flat-leaf) parsley

grated parmesan cheese (optional)

olive oil

FISH STOCK

5 L (4 quarts) water

3 kg (6 pounds) fish heads
without blood or impurities

250 mL (1 cup) white wine

Cook the cannellini beans until tender. This may take up to 2 hours. Cook the potatoes in the same pot — remove when they are ready and peel. Cut into small cubes.

Prepare the fish stock by gently boiling the fish heads with water and a little white wine. This need not be too strong as more fish will be added to the dish later. Strain the fish stock.

Prepare your home-made pasta according to the instructions on page 97. Roll out the pasta on a flat surface with a rolling pin and cut up into 2.5 cm (1 inch) squares as roughly as you can — this provides texture.

Bring the stock to simmering point, add the beans, potatoes, crab and pasta. The pasta will cook quickly, so add the fillets, the prawns and other seafood. (If using clams I prefer to toss them in a little garlic, oil and fresh tomato beforehand and check for sand. If sandy, I put just a few clams in. If fairly clean I put in the lot, including the oil and tomato.)

Finish off with parsley, a little parmesan cheese — I like to break the rules — and a little olive oil does not go astray. A little chilli oil is exciting, as is garlic oil.

ZUPPA DI TRIPPE
TRIPE SOUP

I can hear the loud noises of people complaining that tripe is something horrible, chewy, smothered in something white that they had to eat when they were poor. For others, tripe is an anxiety-causing idea or, at best, an unknown factor.

I beg you to try to cook tripe; handling an ingredient helps to overcome fears about it and the act of cooking itself is a very empowering experience.

If you are going to try it, find a butcher who does not part-cook tripe: it makes it too soft and mushy. You also need time, although very, very little time is actually spent at the stove. Because tripe is slow-cooked, you can do something else once you have the process under way.

There is no point doing a small quantity. This is cheap food that keeps for many days if properly refrigerated.

Serves 10
COOKING TIME: 5–7 HOURS
(HALF IF USING VEAL TRIPE)

3 kg (6 lb) uncooked beef tripe
6 L (5 quarts) chicken or beef stock
3 medium-sized onions, diced
3 medium-sized carrots, diced
2 cups diced celery
3 cloves garlic, diced
olive oil
250 mL (1 cup) white wine
800 g (1 3/4 lb) peeled tomatoes
rosemary
salt and pepper
parmesan cheese

Blanch the tripe even if it looks clean, which it will be. This is just an extra precaution. Cut it in strips thinner than your small finger and set aside.

Warm the stock, which should be strong and clean.

Braise the onions, carrots, celery and garlic in a little olive oil until soft. Add the tripe and wine and cook for a few minutes. Add the tomatoes, cook a while, add the rosemary, salt and pepper, and half of the stock. Keep adding more stock as it evaporates. Cook with a lid on or some aluminium foil over the pot. For the first 3 hours the strips of tripe will be tough as can be. Only after 5 hours do they begin to break down. When they do they are really soft and the sauce becomes creamy.

You can eat tripe with polenta and other vegetables. For soup take the required amount of tripe and add some hot stock and plenty of parmesan cheese. How liquid you wish the soup to be is up to you; I prefer mine not too dense. Some people cook borlotti beans on the side and add them to the soup.

Pastina in Brodo
SHORT AND SMALL PASTA IN BROTH

This recipe is neither regional nor original, and one that I never see celebrated in any literature — books or magazines. Yet the Italians could not live without their pastina in brodo, *a simple and nutritious dish that children actually like a lot. It is easy to prepare and, dare I say, a lot simpler than a number of soups of Asian origin currently in favour now.*

When you go into a store that sells Italian food, take time to see how many types of small pasta there are. Little stars, tiny letters, asterisks, dots, tubes, half tubes, risone, *and so on. The flavour of this soup is as good as your stock. The pasta shapes are cooked in the broth in small quantities because they swell quite a lot. I suggest 1/2 cup of pasta per litre of stock or less.*

Serves 6
COOKING TIME: 20 MINUTES
3 L (2 ½ quarts) chicken stock
1 ½ cups short pasta
1 cup grated parmesan cheese

Bring stock to the boil, then add pasta, cooking until the pasta is *al dente*. Incorporate the cheese and serve at once. You can add shredded meat left-over from the stock to the soup.

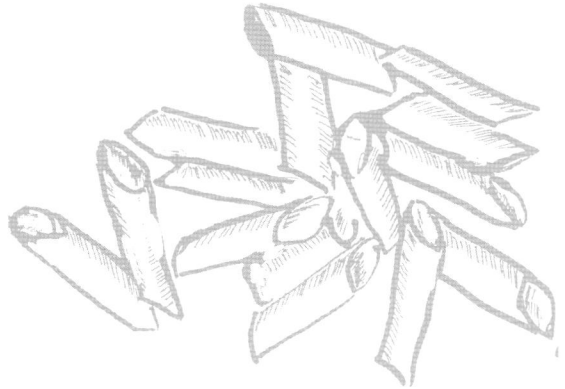

Riso in Brodo
RICE IN BROTH

Once again, a dish hardly ever seen in Australia. The rice is not cooked as in a risotto,
but simply added to a simmering stock and cooked until soft.

I recommend any parboiled rice for this dish as it has a stronger structure which sustains prolonged cooking
in a lot of liquid. The word 'parboiled' is misleading in the sense that people often think that the rice is partly cooked.
In fact, parboiling refers to a method of rice preparation which goes back to antiquity. The rice is first immersed in water,
then steamed at a high temperature. At this point the starch changes from crystalline to gelatine.
The rice is then dried until the water content is at the correct level before being milled as usual
(all rice is brownish in appearance before being polished).

Vitamins and minerals are much higher in parboiled rice than normal white rice.

Serves 4

PREPARATION TIME: NONE
IF YOU HAVE THE STOCK ON HAND

COOKING TIME: 15 MINUTES

2 L (8 cups) strong chicken stock

1 cup parboiled rice

1 cup grated parmesan cheese

Bring stock to the boil, then add the rice. Cook until rice still has a slight 'bite'. Add parmesan cheese to taste.

PASSATELLI IN BRODO
PASSATELLI SOUP

'To go through', or 'to pass' is expressed in Italian by the verb passare, *hence* passatelli, *a simple soup typical of the Romagna region of Italy. You need an implement called a mouli, one with a disk with largish holes. The mouli is placed over the simmering stock and a mixture of egg, cheese and breadcrumbs is pushed through the machine and allowed to fall gently into the stock.*

Do not hold the mouli too close to the stock or the steam will make a mess of things. The passatelli *will expand and cook in the broth in a matter of minutes. I once made an extraordinary dish of* passatelli *with a clear, strong and flavoursome rabbit stock.*

Serves 6
COOKING TIME: 5 MINUTES
(WITH ALL INGREDIENTS TO HAND)
3L (2 ½ quarts) strong chicken stock

PASSATELLI
1 cup breadcrumbs
½ cup good grated parmesan cheese
2 eggs or more
2 teaspoons finely grated lemon zest

Mix all the *passatelli* ingredients in a bowl. If too wet, add more crumbs and cheese. If too dry add an extra egg. This is where common-sense comes in. The mixture must be wet enough to pass through the mouli.

Bring the stock to the boil and set the mouli over the top. Add the *passatelli* mixture and pass through the mouli so that the mixture falls into the stock in 2.5 cm (1 inch) drops. The *passatelli* will expand quickly and are ready in 2–3 minutes.

Serve with additional parmesan cheese at the table.

ON PARMESAN CHEESE AND MILK

Italian food relies significantly on good cheese, and Parmigiano, parmesan in particular. When I use the term 'parmesan' I do so in a generic sense: there are many products with this name on the market. Some are already grated and some are not. Price, as usual, determines what you get. Real parmesan cheese, the authentic McCoy, is something you may use for very special dishes or for special occasions. An alternative to parmesan cheese is Grana Padano. This is similar to Parmigiano-Reggiano but it does not come from within the law-specific zone of production and therefore can be produced in greater quantities without the stringent controls of Parmigiano. One of the things that breaks my heart as a restaurateur is to see good lumps of Parmigiano returning from the dining room on the bottom of the plate, or neatly stacked on the side plate.

If parmesan cheese could be made here it would perhaps be a little more affordable, and the proper thing would enter the national psyche as have other cheese varieties. A combination of bureaucratic stubbornness and vested interests is preventing this development. Australian health regulations prohibit cheese being made with unpasteurised milk. Proper parmesan cheese can only be made with fresh milk.

At this point it is worth recalling one of Philip Hodgins's poems, aptly entitled 'Milk'.

MILK

It's no good any more.
They have treated every last bucketful
so it always tastes the same,
so it never separates
so it rots instead of souring.
My father used to say
Homogenized, pasteurized and buggerized.
And he was right.
They have ruined milk
just to kill a few bacteria
that the bureaucrats couldn't swallow.
And worse than that the ritual's gone.
There's no more going out at first light
to move a hundred drowsy cows
from the warm flattened places
they have created overnight;
to walk them
in the same sequence every time
down the lane
so many hard feet on gravel
the sound of a slow landslide;
and to push them easily into the bails
and strip heavy udders,
the cats coming on time
through the forest of legs

to lick milk off concrete as rough
as their own tongues.
It's not the same
to get up late in the city, find a corner shop
and buy milk that tastes of nothing much.
Back then
the taste of milk
was the lucerne in the spring;
while the worst I ever had
was after the cows got through
a broken fence
and gorged themselves
on the low leaves of excluded peppertrees.
That milk was as sour and bitter
as the leaves themselves
and it was days
before the last trace disappeared.
I hate to think
how many years ago that happened now
but even so
the taste is still strong.
It stays there
a detailed obsession
like the memory of being loved.

PHILIP HODGINS

Sopa Coada

PIGEON BROTH WITH BREAD AND GRANA

Pigeons are now widely available or you can order them from your poultry shop or even through some good butchers.

The Veneto antecedent to this dish is called sopa coada, *where bread, pigeon meat and stock are placed in layers in an earthenware pot and slowly cooked in the centre of the oven. My version is less heavy and fussy.*
Grana Padano cheese is the cheaper parmesan.

Serves 6

PREPARATION TIME: 30 MINUTES
COOKING TIME: 15 MINUTES,
AND 30 MINUTES FOR THE STOCK

6 large pigeons with their livers

1 slice day-old bread per person, preferably a country-style bread

1 cup Grana Padano cheese, lumps the size of a 5-cent piece

best-quality olive oil (optional)

Remove the breasts from the birds and set aside for another use (in a warm salad of breast, for instance). Chop the livers and set aside. Wash the carcasses to remove impurities and blood. Cover with cold water in a stainless-steel pot and simmer for 30 minutes. The resulting stock should be clear. Strain through a cloth to remove any impurities and reduce till the flavour tastes right — usually by half. You must end up with at least 2.5 litres (2 quarts) of stock or more.

Preheat the oven to 180° C (350° F).

Place a layer of bread in an enamelled pot, scatter over the cheese lumps and some livers, and repeat until you have run out of ingredients. (Obviously your pot should not be too wide.) Pour stock over the top and bake for 10 minutes or until the cheese has softened. Once again the ratio of bread to stock must be right. If you are unsure, have some additional stock available, even if made from other poultry. Practice, as cooks know, is the secret of all good cooking.

Ladle the soup into bowls and serve at once. A drizzle of olive oil can help, but it must be good.

Riso e Spinaci
RICE WITH SPINACH

Serves 6

PREPARATION TIME: 40 MINUTES

2–3 L (1 ½–2 ½ quarts) chicken stock

2 cups Arborio rice

2 cups cooked and chopped fresh spinach

good grated cheese, preferably parmesan

salt and freshly ground black pepper

Bring stock to the boil, add the rice and stir from time to time as it cooks. When the rice is nearly soft, add the spinach. Add cheese at the end, and salt and pepper to taste.

The soup should be nicely balanced between rice content and stock with the spinach forming the bridge between the two. If lacking liquid, add some stock. Getting the right consistency comes from practice; it's not a trick that you can learn in a book!

RISI E RISOTTI
RICE AND RISOTTO

Many people eat risotto and are amazed to discover that it was made with rice grown in Italy. In fact, when most people think about Italian food they think pasta; the idea of Italian rice paddies sounds very odd. And yet rice fields there are, vast ones, producing rice that is suitable for soups and risotti. Rice is now planted and harvested mechanically, but once upon a time women called *mondine* manually carried out all operation. If you are old enough, you may remember a classic Italian film with beautiful Silvana Mangano titled *Bitter Rice*. The *mondine* sang all day long and some songs usually contained words not so kind towards the bosses who underpaid them. Rice-growing created a large workforce that gave a strong push to the birth of the Italian Socialist movement.

In Australia the Riviana Company produces rice suitable for risotto. It is very good and I quite like the fact that I have found Riviana Arborio rice in many supermarkets. There is no model risotto, a canonical gastronomy that tells you what to do and what is right and wrong. Risotto can be either dry — in the sense that all liquid has been absorbed — or a little wet, or it can be outright soupy, as in the north-east of Italy.

The important thing about rice — and the varieties of risotto — is to have the intuition to make the right one, having some concern for place, climate and ingredient. In spring, I make a risotto for lunch with asparagus and keep it a little

Risotto ai Funghi (front) (see page 82) and Quaglie Ripiene (rear) (see page 146)

runny. But in the middle of winter I would fancy a rich one with pork sausage.

If you cook a risotto it is best to eat it there and then although, on a hot day, I like it at room temperature. Restaurants specialising in Italian food could perhaps start the tradition of announcing two or three risotti in the course of the evening so that people get a chance to eat them at their best. This requires diners to be a little more flexible and the restaurateur to cop the occasional loss — not a big deal when it comes to rice.

Many restaurants offer reconstituted risotto, that is, partly cooked rice finished off with a particular flavour. I have eaten some truly ghastly ones, so from now on I ask if the rice is cooked to order or from a pre-cooked base. Considering what one pays, at times, one should ask for the best.

I have also found extravagant risotto offerings. As I write the trend is for Peking duck risotto. There is nothing wrong with mixing flavours — I have argued in favour of it right through this book, and in Australia we are free to do what we like. There is, however, decorum, or call it sense of measure, good taste, the fine line between the exquisite and the ridiculous. There are no rules, but the old kiss principle is still the best: Keep It Simple Stupid, especially when it comes to rice.

Risotto requires good, clean stocks. The great interpreter of Italian food for English-speaking palates, Marcella Hazan, writes that stocks should be almost tasteless so as not to interfere with the taste of rice itself and the other principle ingredients. I have followed her advice, but discovered that flavour was lacking. A strong stock will give you a good risotto, that is what my experience has taught me.

Risotto con gli Asparagi
RISOTTO WITH ASPARAGUS

Serves 6

PREPARATION AND COOKING TIME:
40 MINUTES

1 onion, diced

a little garlic

olive oil

3 cups chopped asparagus

2 cups Arborio rice

125 mL (½ cup) white wine

2–3 L (1 ½–2 ½ quarts) clear chicken stock or vegetable stock, hot

parmesan cheese, grated

butter

black pepper

lemon zest and juice

Gently sauté the onion with a little garlic in some olive oil until soft. Add the asparagus and cook a little longer. Add the rice, toast it a bit, then add the white wine to deglaze. Add the stock, a ladleful at a time, until the rice is cooked, about 15 minutes. Add parmesan cheese and butter to taste and sprinkle with black pepper, lemon zest and juice.

You can flood this risotto by adding a little more stock than the rice can take. This will give you a *minestra* which I find delectable.

The practice of introducing asparagus tips towards the end is well-meaning, but you end up with one lot of dull asparagus and one brightly coloured. Up to you. One exciting addition is the introduction of fresh scallops into the risotto towards the end.

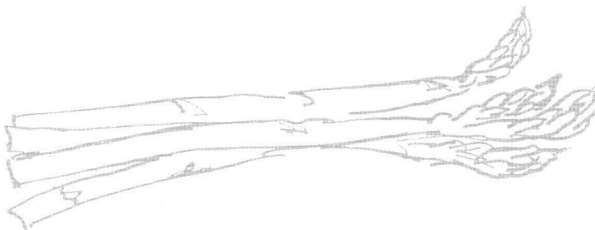

Risotto ai Funghi
MUSHROOM RISOTTO

Serves 6

PREPARATION AND COOKING TIME:
1 HOUR OR LESS

1 tablespoon butter

2 tablespoons olive oil

1 medium-sized onion, chopped

5 cups chopped mushrooms

1 clove garlic, crushed and left whole

3 cups Arborio rice

125 mL (1/2 cup) white wine

3–4 L (2 1/2–3 quarts) chicken or vegetable
stock, hot and ready to go

salt and freshly ground black pepper

parmesan cheese, grated

1/2 cup chopped Italian (flat-leaf) parsley

a touch of lemon zest

a few drops of lemon juice

Have all the ingredients near you and a medium-sized pot ready, preferably a non-stick variety like the enamelled French ones. Failing that, the old faithful aluminium one will do.

Add the butter and olive oil, and fry the onion until soft. Add the mushrooms and garlic, and cook gently for 30 minutes. This is the only way to get some flavour out of the mushrooms, especially if they are of the commercial variety. Even if they look a little too dark, do not worry at all. Remove the garlic.

Add the rice, stir and toast it a bit. Deglaze with the white wine, a bit at a time so as not to lower the temperature. Now start adding the stock, ladle by ladle, stirring all the time in a clockwise direction.

As you go, add a little salt, butter and a handful of parmesan cheese. When the rice is soft — and yet a little firm — it is ready to eat. Turn off the gas, and complete the dish with more butter for creaminess (the rice starches, amylopectins, bind with butter). Add the parsley, more cheese, black pepper and finally that touch of citrus that makes the difference. Let the rice stand in the pot for perhaps 3–4 minutes before serving.

Risotto con Patate e Cipolle
Risotto with Potatoes and Onions

First, the poem.

ODE TO THE POTATO

*O practical
potato,
vegetable,
most like earth,*

*among elegant asparagus,
fashionable aubergine*

*you are unpretentiously
spud.*

*Tasting only of stone
you have nothing to hide,*

*are merely functional
a most puritanical root.*

*Wave your green flags
democratic potato,*

*you the equal
of any other
potato.*

PETER GOLDSWORTHY

Serves 6
PREPARATION AND COOKING TIME:
40 MINUTES

olive oil

1 cup chopped carrots and onions

4 medium-sized potatoes, cut into small cubes

2 cups Arborio rice

125 mL (½ cup) white wine

2–3 L (1 ½–2 ½ quarts) chicken
or vegetable stock, hot

butter

parmesan cheese, grated

Italian (flat leaf) parsley

salt and freshly ground black pepper

Potatoes make a wonderful risotto. You'd think that a farinaceous vegetable with rice would not work so well and yet it does — and it is economical and very practical.

Heat olive oil in a saucepan and cook the carrots and onions and potatoes until they break down.

Add the rice, stir to toast it a little, then add the white wine to deglaze. Add the stock, a ladleful at a time, and stir until the rice is cooked, about 15 minutes.

Take the risotto off the heat and stir through the butter, parmesan cheese and parsley. Season with salt and pepper. Beware: potatoes drink salt so you may end up putting in more than you need to eat. Potatoes also like parsley, so be generous at the end and stir it into the risotto.

Risotto alla Sbirraglia
Risotto with Chicken

This dish is named after the sbirri, *the guards of the noblemen of the past also known as* bravi. *These mercenary soldiers are perfectly described in a wonderful book by Alessandro Manzoni, who is regarded as the second father of the Italian language after Dante Alighieri. In the book,* The Betrothed, *you also get a very good sense of what people ate in the seventeenth century.*

These sbirri *were known for stealing chooks. Whether they simply plucked and threw them into a pot with rice, we don't know, but the legend remains. The chicken is cut in small pieces and cooked with the rice as in a normal risotto. If the chook is good, the risotto will be very flavoursome. With a salad, this is a whole meal. Except, that is, until a few years ago, when* risotto alla sbirraglia *was only the beginning of a long banquet at traditional weddings, and a dish that could make or break the event.*

One of my relatives, a certain Natale Gatto (yes, it translates as Noël Cat or Christmas Cat), was a caterer who specialised in weddings and risotto alla sbirraglia. *Apparently he was good at it but I only remember his big belly and his red nose.*

Serves 8
PREPARATION TIME: 1 HOUR OR LESS

olive oil

1 medium-sized onion, chopped

1 medium-sized carrot, chopped

2 stalks celery, chopped

1 clove garlic, chopped

1 x 1.2 kg (2 lb) chicken, chopped into bite-sized pieces

leaves from a sprig of sage or rosemary

125 mL (½ cup) white wine

3 cups Arborio rice

3–4 L (2 ½–3 quarts) chicken stock or water, hot

butter

salt and pepper

parmesan cheese, grated

Heat olive oil in a deep-sided saucepan and fry the onion, carrot, celery and garlic until fragrant. Add the chicken pieces, the sage or rosemary, and fry until the chicken pieces are brown. Deglaze with the wine, allow the wine to evaporate, and add the rice.

Stir, then add the stock, a ladleful at a time, until the rice is cooked, about 15 minutes.

Take off the heat and stir in the butter, salt and pepper and parmesan cheese.

EELS LIKE BOA CONSTRICTORS

I remember eels appearing on Australian menus in the early 1980s, mostly as a smoked fish for an entrée. A friend of mine, Lorna Hannan, who was born in Gippsland, used to tease and horrify me with tales of gigantic eels at fat as boa constrictors, eels so large that they could attack or chase fishermen. I was more accustomed — as she well knew — to short and slender eels, the sort that you can tie in a knot, roll in flour and deep-fry, or fatter ones that are braised for juicy and sticky dishes to be eaten with white polenta or used in velvety risottos. The thought of great monsters with an inch of fat under their skin put me off eels for a very long time. Chinese restaurants in Australia have rekindled my interest in eels: I love them in black bean sauce, to name just a single dish.

The eels of northern Italy are suitable for slow cooking in a tomato and onion sauce. Their gelatinous content is released through this method of cooking which in the Veneto is called *in tecia*, 'in the pan'. This is the recipe I am providing in this book because I have tested it and I know it can work in Australian conditions. If you are travelling to Venice, find out from your hotel or friends if there is a good place where you can taste eels. In the township of Quinto, near Treviso, there is a restaurant that specialises only in eels.

Part of the fun with eels is to catch them yourself. The most common way, in my time, was to place a system of diminishing concentric nets on the bottom of the stream and against the current. Eels went in but did not know how to turn around and go back the way they had entered. This was the legal way.

The illegal way was to connect metal wires to the power lines, secure them to the end of a pole and lower this makeshift extension into the creek. Dangerous, illegal, immoral, you name it, but so exciting for a young boy! Becoming initiated in this adult activity on a sunny Sunday afternoon when everyone else was having a siesta gave me some of the biggest thrills of my life, perhaps on a par with the day — I was only six years old — my father returned with a cart pulled by his cows loaded with watermelons, or with meeting my first girlfriend. Electricity excites the eels — and other fish — out of their holes and stuns them. It is easy to pull them up with a net. It works if you avoid electrocuting yourself.

Another occasion when I saw eels floating on the creek surface was a July day sometime in the early 1960s. I was helping my father to fertilise the maize by hand. Each plant had to receive its share of something which didn't smell very nice. This was tedious work in the long cycle of polenta production. Mercifully, the rows of corn ended at the creek which was for me a continuous source of distraction. It was really a mini-river with fast running crystal-clear water, not one of those streams that are here now and gone tomorrow. It had a permanent life of water rats, eels, pikes, and other fish whose name I know only in dialect. Thick vegetation grew on its banks, making it even more attractive and mysterious. It was good enough for a swim or for bathing, as in washing one's body, especially after a full day's work in the fields.

As I was squatting on the riverbank to wash my hands and refresh my face, I noticed not one, but ten, twenty, a hundred eels and other fish swimming as close as possible to the surface of the water and flying downstream as fast as fish can go, with an urgency, a sense of purpose or a desperation that only exceptional circumstances could provoke.

At first I was stunned. When I overcame my bewilderment I called out to my father and to my sister Maria to come and see this inexplicable event. By now the fish had become an avalanche of flickering silver sliding down the river. The thought of all that food going past my eyes prevailed over any other consideration. I ran as fast as I could to the neighbours' house where I knew I could borrow a large flour sift and with it I stood in the water at a point where the river was narrowest, caused by the partial collapse of the bank many years before. There I could operate the sift as a giant scoop to intercept the fugitive fish and literally throw the catch up on the bank where others — my father and the neighbours — were chasing the eels before they could escape through the grass and return to the river.

Whatever they caught was placed in buckets and taken to a tub filled with water from the fountain. By the time we had collected enough fish to feed two families for two weeks, news travelled down the river that the fish had been poisoned by some toxic substance released by a factory. Accident or not, we will never know — those were the days when anything was allowed in the name of economic development, and no one dared to question 'progress'.

Dead fish floated for days and days. Hugely inflated eels and swollen pikes making their dead way downstream would be frequently trapped by the thorny blackberry bushes and rot there. I will never forget the stench of death and working in those fields wasn't much fun any more. Sometimes my dad would join me in mournful observation of the dead fish and murmur under his breath, 'Oh, my God, oh my God', but he still refused to view the disaster in political terms.

From then on to the present, not an eel was seen or caught in that river, or any other fish. Those responsible for that type of 'progress' have also been chased from office, flushed out of their safe holes by a wave of public indignation. You could see them running for safety like the eels in my river, but unfortunately it was too late to make a real difference to the country. That type of fish never dies anyway, especially in the Italian political arena where being intoxicated with corrupt power has been a kind of tradition for centuries.

Eels — fortunately — keep living in other waters, some clean and some not so clean, and people go on fishing and eating them as they have always done.

You can get fresh eels from a warehouse in Cubitt Street, Richmond, Victoria, owned by some Chinese people who stock live fish in tanks. No doubt there are similar places in other Australian centres.

I once got my friend, chef Tony Tan, to negotiate the purchase of two incredibly beautiful live eels but even in his best Mandarin he could not persuade them to skin and gut the fish for us. So on a hot summer's day I found myself in Tony's garden late in the afternoon — the garden, that is, of a group of elegant units in salubrious Toorak — doing the job on the slippery eels. As I was washing the blood dripping off the blade of my knife with the garden hose, a little elderly lady stared at me with a very perplexed expression on her face. I had to make up an explanation that would prevent her from calling either the police or the RSPCA. Do make your fishmonger clean the fish or else you will not be able to use it. The rest is easy. For a recipe, see the following page.

Risotto con l'Anguilla

Risotto with eel

I know that mixing cheese and fish is a 'no no' in some quarters but I don't care. I think the cheese adds the necessary creaminess to risotto.

Serves 6

COOKING AND PREPARATION TIME: 1 HOUR

1 small onion, diced

3 cloves garlic, chopped

1 stalk celery, chopped

olive oil

1 kg (2 lb) fresh eel, cut into 5 cm (2 inch) pieces and skinned

125 mL (1/2 cup) white wine

1 x 400 g (14 oz) can peeled Italian tomatoes

salt and freshly ground black pepper

3 cups Arborio rice

2–3 L (1 1/2–2 1/2 quarts) light chicken or fish stock, hot

parmesan cheese, grated

butter

Italian (flat-leaf) parsley

Cook the onion, garlic and celery in a little olive oil until translucent. Add the eel pieces and wine and cook until the wine has evaporated. Add the tomatoes and adjust with a little salt and pepper. Cook until the eel comes off the bone, about 25 minutes.

Take as much cooked meat from the eel as you can and set aside. Press the remaining bones and tomato juices through a sieve. Discard whatever does not go through.

Place the juices in a pot and when hot, add the rice and proceed as for any risotto, gradually adding the stock little by little. Add the remaining eel flesh towards the end, and stir through some parmesan cheese and butter. Sprinkle some parsley over the top before serving. Some people may like a little chilli with this dish.

Risotto con la Salvia e Pesce Persico
RISOTTO WITH SAGE AND FILLETS OF MURRAY PERCH

Living on the Murray River has given me an appreciation of freshwater fish that I had lost after spending almost twenty years in Melbourne. Not that freshwater fish isn't available there: I remember how exotic Murray perch used to appear on one of the displays of a specialist fishmonger at the Victoria Market. My problem was one of being out of focus with freshwater fish and its culinary application.

The risotto with fillets of perch connects loosely with the same risotto in Lombardy where they use pesce persico, which I reckon is very similar to perch in texture, and where sage and butter play a major role in the local gastronomy.

Serves 6

PREPARATION TIME: 30 MINUTES

3 cups Arborio rice

4 oz (120 g) butter

125 mL (½ cup) white wine

2–3 L (1 ½–2 ½ quarts)
light chicken stock, hot

6 fillets Murray perch

plain (all-purpose) flour

12 sage leaves

parmesan cheese, grated

Place the rice in a pot with 3 tablespoons bubbling butter. Add the wine, let it evaporate. Stir, then add the stock, a ladleful at a time, until the rice is cooked, about 15 minutes.

When you are very near the completion of the risotto, place another 3 tablespoons of butter in a frying pan and let it sizzle. Coat the fish fillets with flour and fry in the butter for a short time. Perch fillets cook quickly and are very tender: be careful not to break them when removing them from the pan.

Add the sage leaves to the pan and the remaining butter. Do not worry if the first quantities of butter have browned: all the better.

Pour the sizzling butter and sage over the risotto, which you can place in a nice serving dish, and place the fish neatly over the risotto. Eat at once. This is a very simple, yet delicate, dish, one that combines enough material — perhaps with the addition of a salad — for a complete meal.

It may seem unusual, but a good red wine goes well with this dish.

Risotto con il Pesce Murray Cod
Risotto with Murray Cod

The cod is a fish nature designed to enable us to create our mythologies. It is a beautiful fish to look at, not only when it reaches large proportions, but anytime. When young, its flesh tends to be a little pink. Later, it looks like the colour of pearls. The cod's features are not strange, like those of a catfish, and yet it appears ancient, almost primeval, and it seems to demand a certain respect as a kind of world senior citizen. I loved it at first sight. I am sad whenever I hear that someone has pulled out a big one, and I hope they let the fish go. The idea of knowing that out there, in the depth of some holes, are these huge monsters, is a very reassuring one. What could we say about a world where the big cods have become extinct? What would replace that mythology?

I invite all anglers who catch a big one to photograph, and let it go. I also wish that the morotoria on cod-fishing were extended to at least six months for the next ten years to give the fish a better chance to multiply.

This would be better than the NSW government's decision to buy out all licensed professional fishermen. This is a reaction to anglers' protests that the pros are taking all the fish out of the river. The anglers are the real offenders, as they often catch all kinds of fish of any size, including cod. It is the anglers who get the big cods and do not let them go. The abolition of licences will encourage the growth of an illegal fishing industry as there is no way that people are going to give up what food writer John Newton describes as the fish equivalent of Kobe beef!

Serves 6
PREPARATION AND COOKING TIME:
30 MINUTES

1 cup chopped mixed fennel, onion, carrot and celery

butter

3 cups Arborio rice

125 mL (1/2 cup) dry white wine

400 g (13 oz) cod flesh

2 L (8 cups) chicken stock, hot

a dash of Pernod

butter

parmesan cheese, grated

In a deep-sided saucepan, gently fry all the vegetables in a little butter. Add the rice and the white wine, then add half of the cod and stir through vegetables and rice. Add the stock, a ladleful at a time, until the rice is cooked, about 15 minutes.

Towards the end, add the rest of the cod and the Pernod. Keep going to the end when, as usual, you'll add some butter and parmesan cheese.

Riso con Latte
RISOTTO WITH MILK

*Am I serious? Absolutely. This is a winner when you run out of things in the fridge or on a cold night
or whenever you want to impress the kids. Plain, as a simple white risotto, it makes a great base
for meats that have been stewed for a long time or for the tripe on page 68.*

Serves 6

PREPARATION TIME: 20 MINUTES OR MORE

2 L (8 cups) milk

butter

3 cups Arborio rice

parmesan cheese, grated

2 egg yolks (optional)

squeeze of lemon juice (optional)

salt and pepper

Scald the milk in a saucepan.

Heat the butter in a deep-sided saucepan, then add the rice, stirring to ensure that nothing sticks to the base of the pan. Add the milk, a ladleful at a time, until the rice is cooked, about 20 minutes or more. Season. Rice takes a little longer to absorb milk than stock. This risotto likes extra cheese. For a creamier effect you can add the egg yolks and lemon juice.

PASTA
AND MORE PASTA

Pasta is now such a common component of the Australian diet that I feel uneasy about dispensing recipes for it, but perhaps my way of doing it may complement and expand a little of what you already know.

One thing I am prepared to go on record for is that these days you rarely find a decent plate of pasta in restaurants — pasta that isn't overcooked and not flooded with sauce. Oriental noodles are cooked more than our pastas and are often generously dressed. I love them, but they should not be confused with pasta the Italian way. I feel that, unfortunately, under the rubric 'noodles' anything goes, but often with dubious results.

Those who say that home-made pasta is better than dry pasta should say that the home-made is better for certain types of preparations. Commercially made dry pasta, without egg, has its place in numerous preparations, is cheap, portable, long-lasting, versatile and under-rated. It is not true that it is an inferior type of pasta.

There are very few restaurants out there with the courage to serve a properly cooked bowl of spaghetti — *al dente*, that is — which is an irony in a country where large quantities of pasta are consumed every day. It is not trendy, at the moment, to serve spaghetti also because it has a bad name given to it by generations of pirates in charge of kitchens where speed is all that matters. I understand that a lot of food outlets cannot cook pasta to order because their clientele is not prepared to wait, but there are many others which shouldn't compromise. And the public should be more relaxed and be prepared to wait.

I welcome in this respect the development of the slow food conviviums which are forming in Australia as a move towards the twin pleasures of conversation and sharing a generous table.

Donata, my wife, and I were privileged to be invited to the launch of the South Australian chapter of the slow food movement at St Hallet's Winery. Presided over by the inimitable Bob MacLean, who is as big and generous as his Old Block Shiraz, with food cooked by Maggie Beer and family, the long lunch has remained stuck to my mind. One of the dishes was a perfectly cooked spaghetti dressed with goat's cheese, Italian (flat-leaf) parsley, oil and the odd Sicilian caper. This dish was very pure, simple and direct — a neo-classical dish compared to the opulence of a fettuccine with bolognese sauce.

Pasta Fatta in Casa
HOME-MADE PASTA

This pasta is really indispensable for many soups such as Pasta e Fagioli *(see page 60).*
Its porous nature makes it exceptional for lasagne and cannelloni, fettuccine and tagliolini, spaghetti and tagliatelle —
in short, for sauces that need to integrate well with the given pasta shape. It is also the necessary encasing
for all filled pastas such as ravioli, tortellini and agnolotti.

Briefly, then, we shall describe how to make your own pasta. Many books contain illustrations of all the steps
but if you follow the procedure with common-sense you will not fail.

Serves 6
PREPARATION TIME: 30 MINUTES
3 cups plain (all-purpose) flour
5–6 medium-sized eggs

Mix the ingredients in a large bowl until there isn't any flour left. During this process, some dough will stick to your hands. Wash it off, dry your hands and return immediately to the mixture. I rarely find two batches of pasta to be the same, because of the temperature of the room, because flour is never the same and because of the variations in egg size. Therefore, at this critical point, make sure your dough is not too wet and sticky. If it is, add some more flour and knead it in quite vigorously. If it is too dry, add a few drops of water at a time. Water is a very powerful agent, and it takes very little to make the mixture sticky and slippery. Once you have achieved a smooth dough, keep kneading for several minutes until you are certain that all components are well integrated. Form a ball, cover with a damp cloth and let it rest for a while.

Now set up your pasta machine, giving yourself plenty of space in which to work. Cut off a small piece of dough, flatten it with your hands and start pushing it through the first stage or setting of your machine. Do not handle the dough delicately. Put it through with energy and determination, three or four times, or until you have a regular shape, which is when your sheet is at least as wide as the rollers. It does not matter if it is a little zigzagged at each end, so long as it is as wide as the rollers all the way. This is not for only aesthetic reasons: a regularly shaped pasta sheet minimises waste, especially when making ravioli. To achieve a regularly shaped sheet from the start, do not be afraid to fold the first 'run', as I call it, on itself and push it through several times. If it appears a bit wet, add more flour. Flouring is important all the way to prevent sticking. Do not stack the sheets of pasta on top of each other. If you have a few and you are distracted from your task, you may return to find them stuck together. Once you are through the first setting of the machine, skip one and go on to the next. There is no need to go through each of the six or seven settings to make good pasta.

Proceed in the same manner until you are close to the last setting. At this point you can stop if you intend to cut fettuccine — for which all machines have an attachment — or pappardelle, large strips which you have to cut by hand, or tagliolini, thin strips that you also have to cut by hand. I prefer this second-last setting as the pasta cuts a little thicker than the last which could make it a little gluggy in the boiling water.

For these three shapes, cut your sheet about 30 cm (12 inch) long with a knife on a wide chopping board. Push through the appropriate machine attachment for fettuccine or cut the pappardelle 1 cm (½ inch) wide on the board with a sharp knife. Fold the sheet on itself several times to make cutting easier. If you cut very thin strips — no more than 4 mm (¼ inch) wide — you will obtain tagliolini, which are very good for seafood sauces, tomato-based sauces and even for soups.

If preparing cannelloni or lasagne, proceed all the way to the last setting. These sheets are very delicate and useful for many preparations including vegetarian lasagne, fish-based or meat lasagne. I love a large, delicate pasta sheet as a wrapper for cannelloni with the traditional filling of ricotta and silverbeet.

If you are cutting pasta for lasagne, stay within 10 cm (4 inch) in length. It will expand further when you cook it. With cannelloni, find a length that suits you; I prefer them not too long.

If you want to make spaghetti, some machines have this attachment too, except that the spaghetti will be square rather than round. Don't worry, they round off when cooked. If you like them thin, like angel hair, stay with the second-last setting. If you like them chunky — for a tomato and tuna sauce — take the sheet to the third setting: you'll think it is too thick, but it will go through the cutters and produce marvellous spaghetti.

Lasagna and cannelloni sheets require pre-cooking. Do this in plenty of salted water and when still *al dente*, plunge into cold water to cool briefly and lay out on a clean cloth ready for use. Take time. You are not cooking for an army and you do not have to race the clock. That is the burden of professional cooks.

There is too much emphasis at the moment on *cucina veloce*, the dinner party in 20 minutes. If you are not a confident cook and everyone tells you to be quick, I can see why you surrender to supermarkets and pre-fabricated food.

One of the casualties of fast cooking, and modern cooking, and the new Asian wave, is the old *besciamella* sauce, or *béchamel*. You rarely find a book of Italian cooking that tells you how important this sauce is.

BESCIAMELLA
BÉCHAMEL SAUCE

*Béchamel is very important in the making of lasagne, cannelloni and crespelle, and can also be introduced
into a rich meat sauce to give it a creamy, velvety texture.*

Makes 2 L (8 cups)
PREPARATION TIME: 30 MINUTES
150 g (5 oz) unsalted butter
1/5 cup plain (all-purpose) flour
1.7 L (8 cups) milk, hot
freshly grated nutmeg

Melt the butter and mix with the flour. Cook a little but without browning. Allow to cool and stir in the milk bit by bit, mixing with a wooden spoon. Initially the mixture will be like a gluggy lump but as you add the milk it will break down more and more. Cook it gently for 20 minutes or more, taking care that it does not stick to the bottom of the pan. Do not worry about flavouring the béchamel with onions — it will be incorporated with very strongly flavoured foods.

This recipe should yield a fairly soft sauce, which is what we want. If it is too thick add more milk or water. If you think you have some lumps in it there is no reason to get depressed. Pass it through a fine sieve and everything will be all right.

The obvious partner to béchamel is bolognese sauce, the famous meat sauce which is a must with home-made pasta. This is another old-fashioned delight which is indispensable in Italian cooking.

Bolognese Classica
BOLOGNESE SAUCE

Serves 10 or more, and keeps if refrigerated

COOKING TIME: 3 HOURS

1 carrot, finely diced

1 onion, finely diced

1 stalk celery, finely diced

3 cloves garlic, crushed

enough olive oil to fry gently

400 g (13 oz) minced (ground) quality beef

250 g (8 oz) pork mince, preferably with some fat

250 mL (1 cup) white or red wine

1 x 400 g (14 oz) can peeled Italian tomatoes

1 tablespoon tomato paste

Gently fry the vegetables in the olive oil. When soft, add the meats and then the wine. Let it cook for a while or at least until the liquid content has evaporated. Add the tomatoes and paste, and cook for 2 hours or more.

Spaghetti col Tonno Fresco

Summer Spaghetti with Fresh Tuna

This is a perfect summer lunch with a few friends.

Serves 6

PREPARATION TIME: 30 MINUTES

300 g (10 oz) fresh tuna, cut into strips

3 medium-sized potatoes, boiled and sliced

1 cup diced tomatoes, skin removed

5 anchovy fillets, chopped

olive oil to taste

black olives

chilli (optional)

a pinch of salt

a squeeze of lemon juice

500 g (1 lb) bought spaghetti

1 cup green beans, chopped

Combine all the ingredients except the spaghetti and beans in a large bowl and let them infuse for a while.

Cook the spaghetti in salted boiling water, adding the beans for the last 5 minutes. Drain and pour into the salad. The heat of the spaghetti will cook the raw tuna, which is nice either way.

If you cannot get fresh fish, use a can of tuna with its oil and follow the recipe.

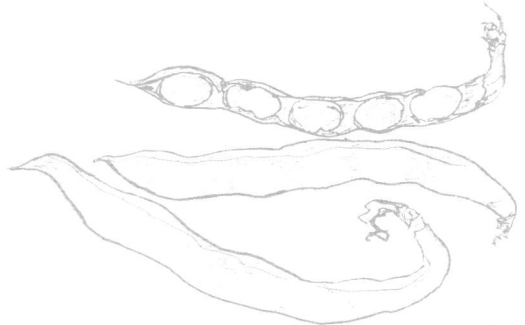

Spaghetti alla Chitarra con Tonno Fresco e Pomodoro

SPAGHETTI 'GUITAR-STYLE' WITH FRESH TUNA AND TOMATO

You can buy, for a few dollars from many specialist food retailers in the major cities, a remarkably simple contraption called la chitarra — a timber frame for a set of strings. You place a 30 cm (12 inch) pasta sheet over the strings, run over it with a rolling pin and the strings cut the pasta, forming flat spaghetti. This is spaghetti alla chitarra, *on the guitar. Get it?*

This pasta is ideal for tomato-based sauces, especially the following one with yellowfin tuna.

The beauty of spaghetti alla chitarra *is that you can regulate their thickness by choosing a pasta sheet that is either thin or thick.*

Serves 4

COOKING TIME: A FEW MINUTES FOR THE SAUCE; 30 MINUTES TO MAKE THE PASTA

350 g (12 oz) spaghetti

good olive oil

a small clove garlic, finely chopped

2 cups diced tomatoes, pips and skins removed

8 thin slices yellowfin tuna, or more

fresh Italian (flat-leafed) parsley

Cook the spaghetti in plenty of salted boiling water until *al dente*.

Heat the oil in a frying pan and add the garlic and tomatoes. Watch — they'll sear and spit and may catch fire, which is not right, and dangerous. Keep a lid at the ready. After the tomatoes have stopped spitting add the tuna, which will cook almost instantly. Whisk off the heat immediately.

Drain the spaghetti and toss them in the pan with the sauce. Add the parsley. Look for a nice balance of sauce to spaghetti. If the spaghetti is a bit dry, add a little olive oil.

Spaghetti con Rucola e Pomodoro
SPAGHETTI WITH FRESH TOMATO AND ROCKET

This is a simple dish that highlights the fantastic versatility of spaghetti. The flavours are very fresh, clean and light, like a perfect summer's day.

Serves 4

PREPARATION TIME: 20 MINUTES

400 g (14 oz) good-quality bought spaghetti

5 tablespoons extra-virgin olive oil

5 medium-sized tomatoes, skinned, seeded and diced

2 cloves garlic, chopped

1 cup chopped rocket (arugula)

salt

parmesan cheese, grated

extra olive oil

Cook the spaghetti in plenty of salted water. Two minutes before it is ready to drain, prepare the sauce. You must have all the ingredients close at hand and move fast.

Heat a large, non-stick frying pan or, preferably, a pot with a wide base. Add the oil, which will be hot in no time. Drop in at once all the tomatoes and garlic. It will sizzle like mad. Make sure if using a frying pan that it does not catch fire (that's why I prefer a large pot with high sides). To avoid fire, place a lid on the pan. Once the tomatoes have released their water they will stop sizzling. This will happen in a minute. Lower the flame a little, add the rocket and a pinch of salt.

Drain the spaghetti — it must be *al dente* — toss in the pan, add some parmesan cheese and, if needed, extra oil.

So much talking about tomatoes in the last few pages! A tomato poem is in order:

TOMATOES

Make no excuse
for the behaviour of tomatoes,
fruit grown soft and fat,
victims waiting for a mouth.

There is no sport in these:
plucking themselves
into the hand, eagerly
consenting to be food.
They give too willingly:
flop-bellies bursting
open, blooding the mouth
unspeakably.

They will never resist.
Kick salt in their eyes,
and pass me another.

PETER GOLDSWORTHY

SPAGHETTI AL GRANCHIO
SPAGHETTI WITH CRAB

The method for this spaghetti with crab is the same as for Spaghetti Con Rucola e Pomodoro (see page 105). Replace rocket with crabmeat and eliminate the cheese. Add some Italian (flat leaf) parsley at the end instead. Allow about 1 cup of crabmeat for 3–4 people. Picking through crabmeat is not so tedious with the help of your family or with a glass of white wine at hand.

You can buy already cooked blue swimmer crab, but if you prepare them yourself, cook them in a large pot of boiling water with about 125 ml (½ cup) white wine and various root vegetables (for example, a stick of celery, a carrot), but don't cook them for more than 5–6 minutes, just enough for the meat to set. After all, you're cooking it again in the pasta.

Spaghetti con Code di Gamberi d'Acqua Dolce
SPAGHETTI WITH YABBY TAILS

Again, the method is as for Spaghetti con Rucola e Pomodoro (see page 105). This time, add cooked yabby tails to the sizzled tomatoes. Think of it as a base, and so do not be scared to add olives and capers.

Spaghetti con Gamberi d'Acqua Dolce
SPAGHETTI WITH WHOLE YABBIES

This requires a good tomato sauce made from standard canned tomatoes (see page 37). It also requires a quantity of cooked yabbies, split lengthwise and cleaned inside. Place them in the tomato sauce and cook a little to integrate the flavours. Add 2–3 cloves (not of garlic, but the spice) and a handful of chopped parsley. Not very elegant eating, but flavoursome.

Bucatini con le Sarde
Bucatini with salted sardines

In the Veneto they have a special device to make a kind of bucatini called bigoi, *a thick spaghetti made with wholemeal flour with a hole in the centre. Commercially available in Australia are bucatini, hollow spaghetti, suitable for a multitude of purposes but perhaps not as popular as other pasta types.*

These bucatini can replace the bigoi, *which was big once upon a time on a Friday in a Catholic country. This dish actually reminds me of a story my friend, Bill Hannan, once told me. During the Great Depression in Melbourne, Archbishop Mannix told the Catholics they were allowed to eat Aussie snags on Friday if they could get hold of any. He didn't think they had any meat in them!*

Obtain salted sardines from any deli and fillet them under running water to remove excess salt. Do not confuse sardines with anchovies!

Serves 4
COOKING TIME: 30 MINUTES
2 onions, finely sliced
butter
olive oil
chicken stock or white wine
10 salted sardine fillets
400 g (14 oz) bought bucatini
Grana Padano cheese
black pepper
fresh herbs (such as Italian parsley), chopped (optional)

Cook the onions in butter and olive oil until they almost caramelise. This will take some time and may need moistening with stock or wine or both, depending on your fancy. When the onions are cooked, add the sardines and smash them with a wooden spoon or a fork.

In the meantime cook the pasta until *al dente*. Drain and toss in a bowl with the sauce. Sprinkle with Grana Padano and black pepper. Add chopped fresh herbs if you like.

Tagliatelle con Piselli Freschi
Tagliatelle with Fresh Peas

When you come across some fresh and tender peas, do not let the opportunity of making this delicious pasta pass you by. You may well ask: do I have to make pasta by hand every time I fancy something? Well, the Italian mammas of old used to make it twice a day in some households, but you have the freezer. So, when you make a batch, cut the pasta into the different shapes and place it in pizza boxes: they stack neatly in the freezer. Pasta thus preserved loses some of its romantic appeal but makes life a lot easier without affecting its quality.

Serves 4
COOKING TIME: 30 MINUTES

1 small onion, chopped
butter
olive oil
water or chicken stock
250 g (8 oz) fresh shelled peas
350 g (12 oz) fresh home-made tagliatelle
thickened cream
extra butter
salt and freshly ground black pepper
parmesan cheese, grated

To cook the peas, cook onion with butter and a little olive oil in a non-reactive pan. Add the peas, cover with water or a little stock and cook with the lid on until soft.

Cook the tagliatelle in salted boiling water until *al dente*.

Melt some butter in a pan, add the peas and cream and cook for a few moments. Add salt and pepper to taste. Drain the tagliatelle, toss with the sauce and parmesan cheese.

This base (not with the cream) will make a risotto.

TAGLIATELLE AL CARCIOFO E PARMIGIANO
TAGLIATELLE WITH ARTICHOKES AND PARMESAN

Around Mildura, where I live, you can tell an Italian farmhouse straight away by the silvery artichoke plants at the end of each row of vines. For me, nature could not have made a better vegetable. Alas, for a lot of diners it remains a mysterious, clumsy and even intimidating thing to eat. Once again, this has to do with where one grew up. A large part of my food memories is taken up by the image of mountains of artichokes being cut up in the market of Treviso by deft hands preparing the fondi di carciofo, *the bottoms of artichokes which are tender and nutty in flavour. These were dropped into huge ceramic bowls (patterned on the inside with green streaks) along with water, lemon slices and parsley stalks.*

Serves 4

PREPARATION TIME: 10 MINUTES

COOKING TIME: 10 MINUTES
IF THE ARTICHOKES ARE READY

1 full cup (approximately 4) artichokes without hard leaves

water

lemon juice

1 bunch Italian (flat-leaf) parsley

chicken stock

250 mL (1 cup) cream

350 g (12 oz) home-made tagliatelle

½ cup grated parmesan cheese

freshly ground black pepper

To prepare the artichokes, remove the outer leaves and cut off and discard most of the stem. Peel the remaining stem and cut off about 1 cm (½ inch) of the leaf tips. (When handling artichokes wear gloves or they will stain your hands.) Drop the cleaned artichokes into water with lemon to prevent discolouration as you go, and cook them in a stainless-steel pot to prevent further discolouration

Heat some oil and garlic, but do not let it burn. Place the artichokes in the pot and cover them with a large quantity of parsley and enough chicken stock to cover them evenly. Put a lid on the pot and turn the heat to medium-low. Cook for about 1 hour or until soft and take off heat.

Remove the artichokes from the pot when cold and detach any remaining hard leaves. Chop the soft core into small pieces.

Mix the cream with the chopped artichokes and gently warm.

Cook the pasta until *al dente*. Drain, sprinkle with cheese and toss in the sauce. Serve at once with black pepper.

This base (not with the cream) will make a risotto.

Rigatoni con Tuorli, Pomodoro e Cannella

RIGATONI WITH EGG YOLKS, TOMATOES AND NUTMEG

This recipe requires close attention to the balance of the components or else it will fail.
The nutmeg makes it very exotic and the eggs creamy.

Rigatoni are the large pasta tubes with ridges all around.

Serves 4
COOKING TIME: 40 MINUTES, INCLUDING
TIME TO MAKE A TOMATO SAUCE
500 mL (2 cups) standard, home-made
Tomato Sauce, at room temperature
(see page 37)
4 egg yolks
1 teaspoon (or more) freshly grated nutmeg
best-quality parmesan cheese, grated
350 g (12 oz) bought rigatoni

Place the tomato sauce in a bowl large enough to hold the pasta later. With a fork blend in the yolks, nutmeg and cheese to taste.

Cook the rigatoni in plenty of salted water until *al dente*. Drain and toss in the sauce.

Farfalle con Crema di Peperoni
FARFALLE WITH CAPSICUM CREAM

I think this is an ancient recipe lost in the midst of nouvelle cuisine times, but it is a favourite of mine and not one that I have encountered often.

Serves 4

COOKING TIME: 40 MINUTES

1 onion, chopped

2 cloves garlic, chopped

4 tablespoons olive oil

5 fleshy red capsicums (bell peppers), sliced and seeds removed

a few whole basil leaves

250 mL (1 cup) chicken stock

125 mL (½ cup) cream

350 g (12 oz) bought farfalle (bow ties)

½ cup Grana Padano cheese, grated

black pepper

Cook the onion and garlic in olive oil in a pot until transparent. Add the capsicums, basil and the stock. Cook with the lid on for 15 minutes or until soft.

Purée in a food processor, return to the pot and add the cream. Warm this while you cook the farfalle in salted boiling water until *al dente*. Drain, add to the sauce, add cheese and serve at once with black pepper.

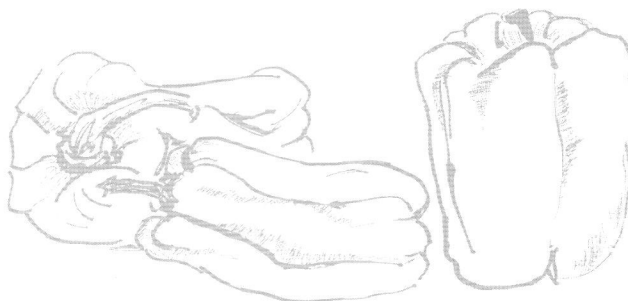

Pappardelle al Sugo di Coniglio
PAPPARDELLE WITH RABBIT SAUCE

Country people call rabbit underground mutton and they are not all that fond of it. I must say that rabbits, when they come from the wild, vary a lot in quality. One way of having your rabbit — without having to eat it if you do not like it or if it is too tough — is to use it as a sauce flavouring for the pappardelle. The recently introduced virus has not yet wiped out rabbits and where it has, I'm sure they will come back. I reckon the most sensible solution to the rabbit problem is to keep on cooking them.

Serves a generous 6
PREPARATION TIME: 2 HOURS

olive oil or lard for frying

2 cups coarsely chopped root vegetables

2 cloves garlic

1 rabbit, cut into pieces

125 mL (½ cup) white wine

2 x 400 g (14 oz) peeled and crushed Italian tomatoes

a pinch of rosemary leaves

black olives (optional)

500 g (1 lb) home-made pappardelle

extra olive oil

parmesan cheese, grated

This is a basic list of ingredients. Herbs can be changed or added, depending on what you have. Use a heavy pot, or one of those French enamelled ones.

When the oil or lard is hot, drop in the root vegetables and garlic and cook them until soft. Add the rabbit pieces. (Some would suggest that you lightly dust the rabbit with flour and fry it in a separate pan before adding it to the pot.) After you have added the rabbit, deglaze with the wine, add the tomatoes and herbs, and put the lid on. Lower the flame and go and do something else. Return occasionally to check that things have not stuck; add a little stock or water if things are getting too thick. After a couple of hours the tomato should have a strong rabbit flavour and if the rabbit itself is soft, you may well eat it, or else fish it out and give to your pets.

Cook the pappardelle in plenty of salted water until *al dente*. Drain, and dress with the sauce. Add some extra olive oil and parmesan cheese.

Pappardelle con i Fegatini

PAPPARDELLE WITH CHICKEN LIVERS

Chicken livers are readily available, nearly always fresh, and are inexpensive. Combined with a small amount of cream and the flavour of sage, they make an exquisite partner for the pasta ribbons known as pappardelle.

Serves 4

PREPARATION TIME: 30 MINUTES

1 small onion, finely diced

1 clove garlic, finely chopped

4 tablespoons butter

1 tablespoon olive oil

8 sage leaves

250 g (½ lb) fresh chicken livers

salt and pepper

125 ml (½ cup) cream

500 g (1 lb) home-made pappardelle

parmesan cheese, grated

Sauté the onion and garlic in butter and oil until golden. Add the sage and chicken livers and season with salt and pepper. Cook livers until pink inside. Add cream and reduce a little.

In the meantime cook the pappardelle in salted water and when *al dente* drain and add to the sauce. Finish with cheese and stir to mix the sauce through.

Lasagna Tradizionale
TRADITIONAL LASAGNE

I love lasagna. It may not be fashionable any more, but good lasagna is a winner with kids and adults alike. There is a ritual involved here — the making of home-made pasta, the making of the béchamel and the patient preparation of the bolognese sauce, or ragù alla bolognese.

I love the white linen on which the pasta sheets are placed to rest before they are cooked, the bits of flour everywhere, the smell of the simmering meat on the stove and the ritual of eating some with bread before the lasagna is finally put together. I would like to imagine families being involved in this process on a Sunday morning, or at holiday time. It may be I am a hopeless romantic.

Serves 12
PREPARATION TIME: 2 HOURS
IF PREPARING SAUCES
COOKING TIME: 20 MINUTES

2 L (8 cups) Bolognese Sauce (see page 101)
1 L (4 cups) Béchamel Sauce (see page 100)
500 g (1 lb) home-made pasta sheets
(see page 97), cooked
parmesan cheese, grated
200 g (7 oz) shredded mozzarella

Preheat the oven to 180°C (350°F).

Place some bolognese sauce and béchamel on the bottom of a large baking dish, place a layer of pasta over it, then sauce, béchamel, parmesan cheese and mozzarella. Add another layer of pasta and continue until you have filled the baking dish or have run out of ingredients, keeping enough béchamel for the top layer.

Bake in the oven for 30 minutes until it has formed a light crust. I find that lasagna is better made a day before. It takes to reheating without problems.

LASAGNETTA DI VERDURE
VEGETABLE LASAGNA

I l ke home-made vegetable lasagna. Done with care, it is great when lots of vegetables are available. As quantities here may vary — it is never worth making a small one — I will not give measurements.

1 quantity of home-made lasagna sheets
(see page 97)

fresh home-made Tomato Sauce (see page 37)

eggplant (aubergine), cut into matchsticks
and lightly fried in a light olive oil

zucchini, cut into matchsticks
and lightly blanched

carrots, cut into matchsticks
and lightly blanched

boiled potatoes, thinly sliced

shredded mozzarella

parmesan cheese, grated

ricotta cheese, crumbled

a quantity of light béchamel sauce
(see page 100)

BASIL PESTO
½ cup pinenuts
2 whole cloves garlic
2 cups young, tender basil leaves
250 mL (1 cup) olive oil
½ cup grated parmesan cheese

Preheat the oven to 180°C (350°F).

In a baking dish prepare the lasagne layer by layer—but not more than four, otherwise it is too stodgy—alternating all the ingredients. Use the potatoes for the bottom layer and do not forget to salt as you go as all elements are not strongly flavoured. Keep a layer of béchamel for the top. Bake for 30 minutes. Serve with pesto drizzled over the top.

To make the pesto, place the pinenuts in the food processor with garlic. Whiz until all are broken down. Add basil leaves, whiz and add oil at the same time. (Light Ligurian oil is the best.) When you have obtained a nice, runny paste, you are done. Add parmesan cheese to the pesto only when you are using it. The rest of the pesto keeps in the fridge in a jar as long as it is covered with oil. (For best results avoid Chinese pinenuts. They have a different flavour.)

THE SOUNDS OF THE YARD

My family was one of three that occupied the same house, the house that was once a summer residence for a Venetian bishop. The whole property, which was once ruled over by my great grandfather, eventually split three ways. My father found himself with one of the three parts, which means that he had one of three pig sties, one of three sheds, a third of a stable, a third of the granary, and so on. Because there were many of us under the same roof and all were doing much the same thing as nature dictated, there was great physical proximity — not always a blessing, I must say — which called for a great amount of tolerance.

My brother was practising piano all night for many years in a hall in the centre of the house which gave access to four of the bedrooms in the main building. Each room was occupied by a young couple and I am sure that many children were procreated to the sound of Chopin who, in turn, had to compete with some solid snoring.

It was during the day that I enjoyed watching what was going on in the yard where communal activities took place and where all kinds of fights exploded. The Swan, for instance, used to imbibe a little too much and his wife would deny him any services during the afternoon — if you know what I mean — as a form of punishment, which used to send him raging.

'You bitch, you cow, you mean …' and much more that I cannot repeat, said in a much more colourful language.

My mother's wash-up room was adjacent to Swan's wife's and they communicated through a small window.

'Don't make him rage,' my mother would say.

'I can't stand it when he drinks,' came the reply.

The best sounds were our voices just before a storm threatened to pour bucketfuls over the carts loaded with hay.

'Quick, push the son of a bitch under the shed, quick, hurry up,' and more unspeakable exhortations, and blasphemies galore. My parents never blasphemed, but others did as it is quite 'normal' in the most religious parts of Italy. Abuse was hurled against God in terms that would make you cringe with shame and embarrassment.

On the other hand, my parents were rather religious, so if a hailstorm threatened, out came the candles and dried olive branches and bucketfuls of prayers and implorations to all the

Saints — St Agnes was a favourite for a while and later on St Rita — to stop the hail. Alas, when God made up His mind that it would be hail the size of walnuts, no Saint could stop Him and much damage was wreaked.

In 1954 trees were stripped of all their leaves and after the storm looked as naked as they do in the winter. That caused a total loss of corn and grapes, two major staples in the district. So you could hear a stream of Hail Marys from one kitchen while in another the disaster was followed with implacable silence. I have learnt that for the religious peasant God continues, even after the hail, as a form of consolation and hope called faith. For the secular one, anger builds up with nowhere to go.

My father abandoned all his reserve and gentle manners twice daily: at 8 a.m. when his breakfast was never ready. What he said I cannot repeat because the word 'cow' in English is very specific and cannot be applied as liberally as in Italian. Why my mother delayed that breakfast I will never comprehend. After all, they had both been up since about five o'clock. And at six in the evening, she never had the milk pails washed and ready for the milking. Thereupon my father would explode: 'I have worked like a dog all day, all I ask is that you have the pails ready, and they never are, never. You must do it on purpose, you …'

'Shut up you cretin … I have worked a lifetime to serve you, and your family, blah blah blah …'

The main commotion came with the threshing machine, when mountains of wheat were amassed in the yard and guarded overnight in case of fire or rain. Threshing would begin in earnest before sunrise: the big red machine, something that looked like an awesome work of art to me, was given life by the orange Fiat tractor and until all the wheat had been separated work went on in a perfect geometry of technology, skill and physical strength.

On top of the mountain of wheat were the women who fed the machine. Bales of straw came out of one end and it took the skill of the older blokes to build, block by block, a stack that would be covered with a straw roof. The younger and stronger men carried the sacks of wheat on their shoulders up to the granary, three flights of stairs, a cigarette dangling from their lips.

By 3 p.m. everyone had a black face and was exhausted. The girls went to wash in the stream under the bridge and the blokes shared soap around the pump and the trough. There was an air of festivity, not only because the work was finished, but also because the working day stopped there — save for feeding the cows later.

Everyone then sat at a long table with bread and carafes of wine and water to be served what was called the 'wheat lunch', consisting of lots of salads, cooked vegetables, tortellini in *brodo*, boiled chicken (*capon*) and sponges with custard. I still have in my mouth the taste of boiled meat and *giardiniera*, the pickled vegetables that went out of fashion years ago.

Even though we do not thresh wheat any more, my brothers, sisters and cousins still meet once a year for a wheat dinner. It is just an excuse for a night of nostalgia for things lost.

Now I live in a region called the Mallee where wheat is the main farming activity. As I drive into Melbourne late in the evening in the early summer I see harvesting machines slowly chewing up yellow paddocks that stretch from one side of the horizon to the other. As they light up to work into the night, I tell my sleepy children that they are fireflies.

Ravioli di Casa
HOME-MADE RAVIOLI

Making your own filled pasta (see page 97) gives you a sense of satisfaction and achievement. Once you have mastered the art of pasta you will find making your own quite irresistible. The important thing is being able to roll out regular sheets with your machine. I suggest that you work with just one sheet at a time. Once stretched — and for me, the thinner the better — cut the pasta sheet in half. Put one half aside and on the other, place two lines of filling at regular 2 cm (3/4 in) intervals. Brush some egg yolk on the other pasta sheet and place over the filling, making sure when you seal it that no air pockets form. Once this task is completed, sprinkle generously with flour and cut with the appropriate implement.

When cooking ravioli, use the same procedure as for cooking any other pasta. But do make sure that the pasta is cooked where the two sheets of dough have been pressed together.

This dough is also suitable for wrapping wontons.

Ravioli Ripieni di Granchio
Blue Swimmer Crab Ravioli

Serves 10

PREPARATION TIME: 2 HOURS
COOKING TIME: 10 MINUTES

2 kg (4 lb) blue swimmer crabs
1 whole onion
1 whole stick celery
10 whole peppercorns
250 mL (1 cup) white wine
5 stalks parsley
125 ml (½ cup) cream
fine black pepper
300 g (10 oz) pasta dough (see page 97)
butter
salmon roe (optional)

Cook the crabs in a stock made with water, onions, celery, peppercorns, white wine and the parsley stalks. There has to be enough liquid to cover the crabs. Do not cook for more than 5 minutes.

When cool, crack open with nutcrackers and remove the white meat. The handle of a teaspoon is also useful for getting to the tricky parts of the crab. Add just enough cream to the meat to bind it and a little fine black pepper. But don't make it too wet or else it will dampen and ruin the pasta.

Make the ravioli and follow the instructions on page 123 for wrapping. Cook in salted boiling water until the ravioli float to the surface. Drain.

Dress with butter, with salmon roe, or whatever takes your fancy. Ultimately, I always prefer to taste the natural, straight flavour of the crab.

Ravioli Ripieni di Quaglia
Ravioli with Quail Filling

Serves 10

PREPARATION TIME: 2 HOURS
COOKING TIME: 10 MINUTES

cup chopped vegetables, for example
onion, carrot, celery and a little garlic

butter

8 quails, deboned, breasts only

1 egg

½ cup grated parmesan cheese

½ cup breadcrumbs

a little parsley

a little grated lemon zest

300 g (10 oz) pasta dough (see page 97)

butter

sage

extra parmesan cheese, grated

Cook the vegetables in a pan with a little butter. Add the quail breasts, and cook for about 2 minutes until they turn pink. Place the lot in a food processor and process to a fairly fine paste. Add the egg, parmesan cheese, breadcrumbs, parsley and lemon zest. This mixture should not be too wet or it will make a mess of your pasta. Nor should it be too dry.

Make the ravioli and follow the instructions on page 123 for wrapping. Cook in boiling salted water until the ravioli float to the surface. Drain.

For the sauce, make a stock by simmering the remaining quail carcasses in a covered baking dish with some root vegetables in a 180°C (350°F) oven for 2 hours. Strain and cook again until only ½ cup of concentrated stock remains. That concentrated essence is good combined with a little butter, sage and parmesan cheese.

POETRY IN THE KITCHEN

There is an Italian gentleman who has been helping me in my kitchen for some time. His name is Leopardo Leopardi or Leopardo Ottavio Maria Leopardi, Conte di San Leopardo, to be precise. Leo, as he is simply called by his colleagues, is a charming and intelligent man who really understands Italian flavours.

Like many other music graduates in Italy in the 1950s, Leopardo could not get a serious job in his field. My own brother, for example, faced with the same predicament, came to Australia where he established himself teaching organ.

Leopardo could not go very far with his trombone. After a stint with the Swiss Symphony Orchestra, he became disillusioned with professional music-making and chose to become a chef. I was fortunate to become his friend and it is through this friendship that he has come to Mildura to help me.

Leopardo is also a direct descendant of the celebrated Italian poet Giacomo Leopardi. Together with Alessandro Manzoni, Giacomo Leopardi is compulsory reading and memorising in Italian schools.

Giacomo's life almost overlaps chronologically with that of Schubert. Both were shortlived and in Giacomo's case, bitter and miserable. Giacomo did not write only beautiful poems, he left us with a book of his thoughts, a collection of short moral, ethical, aesthetic and philosophical statements.

One of these — which Giacomo wrote with literary composition in mind — has a remarkable application to cooking. I have broadly paraphrased it so as not to ruin by bad translation his flowing prose.

So he who wishes to express the mood of his heart, the last thing he will achieve is simplicity and natural[ness]. And his first achievements will be artifice and affectation [and] he who had not studied and read is innocent, but will not write with simplicity, but in the opposite style. The height of art is to be natural and to hide art itself. The beginners or the ignorant do not know how to hide it, and the little they possess they let it transpire which is as revolting as it is crude.

Strozzapreti di Leo
Leopardi's Priestchokers

This pasta dish that I learnt from Leo is made without eggs, which makes it different from the ones before. Plain (all-purpose) flour and water are gradually mixed to form a soft, silky dough.

I will not give you quantities because flour is always different, as are the conditions in which you work it. Only practise will give you this very traditional pasta but a ratio of 2 parts flour to 1 part water (or less) should provide the right proportions. And if you use 500 g (1 lb) flour and 250 mL (1 cup) or less of water, added gradually, you should make enough pasta to serve six people. Take the dough to the last notch of your machine and cut it into strips 1 cm wide by 5 cm long (1/2 inch by 2 inch). Roll these one at the time between the palms of your hands so that they roll on themselves and look a little like a screw. This is the simplest way of describing this delectable pasta dish which is best dressed with a bolognese-type sauce (see page 101).

This dish is traditional in areas that were anticlerical, that resented being under papal rule. In the popular imagination *strozzapreti* were meant to choke the parson who invited himself to dinner too often. The intentions of the cook and the dish are rather clear. I do not know if this dish ever contributed to the diminution of the number of clergymen, but I doubt it because the dish is so good that the priest would have come back for more!

Strozzapreti must be cooked in plenty of salted water and be used immediately — combined flour and water can become harder than a rock when dry. If unable to use immediately or if you want to prepare ahead, you must freeze them.

PENNE LISCIE AL FORNO
BAKED PENNE

*This is a dish for late summer when Roma (plum) tomatoes are cheap and very, very ripe.
Read on because it is not the usual recipe.*

Penne are short, smooth pasta tubes.

Serves as many as 10
PREPARATION TIME: 30 MINUTES
COOKING TIME: 40 MINUTES
1 kg (2 lb) penne
500 mL (2 cups) extra-virgin olive oil
3 kg (6 lb) ripe Roma (plum) tomatoes, skinned, seeded and chopped
2 cups grated Parmigiano-Reggiano
salt
½ cup torn basil leaves
2 cups cubed mozzarella

Place the uncooked penne in a 40 x 30 cm (16 x 12 inch) baking dish and pour over the oil. Stir from time to time; in a few hours they will have absorbed most of the oil. Keep turning them so that they do not dry out.

Preheat the oven to 180°C (350°F).

Add the tomatoes and Parmigiano to the baking dish. Toss and add salt as you go — a good sprinkle is necessary.

Cover with aluminium foil and bake for 45 minutes or until cooked. Check after 25 minutes to ensure that the penne are still moist, that you do not need more tomato and the top is not too dry. I advise you to stir the penne with a spoon. Taste for salt and return to the oven. This dish should taste fresh and creamy. Some basil and fresh mozzarella on top will finish the dish.

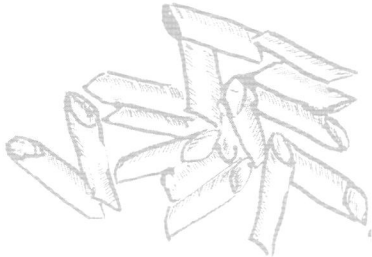

Gnocchi di Patate
POTATO GNOCCHI

One of the great dishes of northern Italy, perhaps on a par with risotto. This is such a classic dish it is easy to distinguish a good 'hand' from a bad one. A good plate of gnocchi is founded on two premises: the first, that the gnocchi must be soft, almost airy, and potato tasting; the second, that the sauce must be completely satisfying — rich but not so overpowering as to mask the taste of the potato.

If the potato is very wet and you use too much flour you will end up with small rocks. Never overwork the pastry or you will make the mixture gooey.

When you make gnocchi go after the older potato; spuds with a lower water content.

Soft flour is the other ingredient, a pinch of salt and, for me, no eggs, although people find one or two acceptable. Have a pot of boiling water at the ready: make a few gnocchi and test them. If they do not spoil in the water, you can go ahead, because it means that you have enough flour to keep the mixture together.

I do not like gnocchi in tomato sauce. I prefer a rich meat sauce like a classic bolognese (see page 101) or the sauce from a 'brasato', although I admit that burnt butter and sage has a certain elegance and definition.

Serves 6 or more people
PREPARATION TIME: 1 HOUR
1 kg (2 lb) old potatoes (or pink eye)
a pinch of salt
½ cup or less plain (all-purpose) flour

Boil the potatoes on a rack on the bottom of the pot so that they are raised at least 2.5 cm (1 inch) from the bottom of the pot. Use a lid to trap the steam inside. Do not undercook. Peel. Use a ricer if you can find one — even the old faithful mouli can develop the starches above the acceptable point — and pass the potatoes through.

Form a mound on the table and sprinkle with a little salt. Sprinkle some flour over the potato and quickly blend it in without overworking. I cannot be more precise because I would like you to use as little flour as possible. Trial and error will give you the confidence to know when enough is enough.

Cut a small quantity from the mixture and roll out like mini-*salame*: cut into pieces no longer than

2.5 cm (1 inch) and not thicker than a thumb. Cook a few in boiling water to see if they fall apart. If they do, sprinkle more flour and do not be too alarmed. Do not concern yourself at this stage with rolling the gnocchi on the back of a fork to cause the indentations that are supposed to pick up the sauce: leave that for when you have perfected gnocchi making.

When ready, the gnocchi will rise to the surface. Scoop them out with a colander and place either in a saucepan with sauce or directly on the plate if you wish to pour the sauce over it.

Remember to work swiftly and use your fingertips. Making gnocchi is like walking on hot coals, it is like thinking on tiptoes or walking softly so as not to wake up your lover.

RAVIOLI DI PATATE E BOLOGNESE
RAVIOLI OF POTATO AND BOLOGNESE

Gnocchi remind me of a good mash flavoured with parmesan cheese. There is an old recipe where potato purée is mixed with bolognese sauce. This becomes the filling for a ravioli which, in turn, is dressed with bolognese.

It is not starchy if your hand is light. A terrific idea for leftovers, although I think it is worth doing just for its own sake.

Serves 10

PREPARATION TIME: 1 HOUR IF PASTA
AND BOLOGNESE SAUCE ALREADY
PREPARED; IF NOT, 3 HOURS IN TOTAL

300 g (10 oz) pasta dough (see page 97)

750 mL (3 cups) Bolognese Sauce
(see page 101)

300 g (10 oz) mashed potato
(preferably leftovers)

1 cup grated parmesan cheese

Combine half the bolognese sauce with the mashed potatoes until smooth.

Roll out the pasta dough following the method given on page 123 and fill the ravioli with mixture.

Cook the ravioli in boiling salted water. Drain. Then dress with the remaining bolognese sauce (which has been heated) and parmesan cheese.

Gnocchi di Ricotta
Ricotta Gnocchi

This is a light dish and good vegetarian fare. Here a quantity of ricotta is mixed with grated parmesan cheese and flour. Again, use as little flour as possible. Do not even attempt to make this dish out of the ricotta in the small tubs — it's usually very wet. Use instead fresh ricotta from the large rounds that you see in delis. Being a little drier, the ricotta will take less flour.

If you want to be extra smart, mix in some finely chopped cooked spinach. If you do so, you will need fewer eggs. Once these gnocchi are cooked, they can be placed in a baking dish and cooked as a gratin. They are very versatile as they can absorb a fair bit of liquid sauce.

Ricotta gnocchi are also good when served with gorgonzola (an elegant blue cheese). With the ricotta and parmesan you are actually making a gnocchi with three cheeses.

Serves 6
PREPARATION TIME: 30 MINUTES
2 cups ricotta
½ cup plain (all-purpose) flour
2 eggs
½ cup grated parmesan cheese

SAUCE
6 tablespoons gorgonzola
6 tablespoons butter
250 mL (1 cup) cream

Blend the ricotta gradually with the flour and eggs, without overworking. As with potato gnocchi, the trick is to avoid making the mixture too wet.

Cut a small quantity from the mixture and roll out like a mini-salame: cut into pieces no longer that 2.5 cm (1 inch) and not thicker than a thumb. Cook a few in boiling water to see if they fall apart. If they do, add a little more flour to the mixture.

When ready, the gnocchi will rise to the surface. Scoop them out with a colander.

To make the sauce: blend the gorgonzola, butter and cream in a food processor, then melt in a frying pan. Add the gnocchi to the sauce and finish with a small amount of parmesan cheese.

COUSIN BERTO AND THE
VANISHING POT OF OYSTER MUSHROOMS

As a kid I loved oyster mushrooms for two reasons: they were rare and they fetched top *lires*. Oyster mushrooms grew in the wild on rotten poplar, mulberry and willow stumps, but not on all stumps. Special conditions had to be right for the appearance of these black and white aristocrats, and rarity and prestige go together, as we know. The respected mushroom hunters had to have a few secret spots for oyster mushrooms in their CVs to gain their quasi-mystical aura and consequent special status in the community.

I once jumped off my brother's Vespa travelling at some speed upon spotting out of the corner of my eye and for a split second a stump covered in mushrooms that had been there for all passers-by to see: such is the power of mushrooms that they can be there and you cannot see them. Mind you, real hunters can nose them, so to speak, dig them out with their will, make them materialise and grow in funny places — in a patch of stinging nettles, or on a stump supporting the neighbour's gate or inside a hollow trunk or on the side of the road or near a bus stop. Tales of mushroom findings are as infinite as the possibilities for their growth.

Cousin Berto and Uncle Gigio did not have to move a finger to obtain oyster mushrooms; they had not one, but several dead poplars laden with mushrooms at the back of their house, inside a fenced-off area that kept in various chickens, turkeys and so on. The back door of their huge kitchen faced the chook yard. Through the glass or the open doors you could see and almost touch these mushrooms. The mushrooms had an unusually special effect on me — please do not laugh! — the mere sight of these things would alter my mind, stir up the frustrated hunter and collector instinct, not to mention the anger and jealousy I felt towards my privileged relations. What made matters worse was that they never offered that I go and pick a couple.

Cousin Berto was an opera lover. Year after year all opera seasons would be his. He would get on his bike for the Treviso Rail Station, then a second-class return trip to Venice, 25 minutes by foot to the Teatro Gran Fenice and all that in reverse around midnight. At four in the morning he was at the factory removing bricks from the kilns and back home at 2 p.m. to collect oyster mushrooms. That is how I saw him and that is how I remember him.

One day the cocktail of anger and frustration got the better of me and I broke into the enclosure at dusk. With the cover of the evening blue and a spittle of rain I committed my first and only burglary: I stole the mushrooms, a whole hatful, picked discreetly here and there so that the crime would pass unnoticed and could be repeated. I retreated from the scene of the crime with a pounding heart, ridden with an emulsion of guilt, revenge and satisfaction, shame and joy. It was a Saturday evening and I got home late, wet and smelling of chook poo.

Mum said, 'Where did you get these mushrooms? Not from your uncle's chook yard, I hope?'

My heart sank at being almost discovered.

The following morning being Sunday, Mum started cooking early as usual. She prepared a nice casserole of oyster mushrooms which she left on the side of the stove with a lid on top to be used later as a risotto base. At about 11.30 a.m., just half an hour before lunch, cousin Berto rocked up on his bike.

'Hi aunt, I came to see how you are going,' he said, while I busied myself with the task of grating cheese.

'Hi, Berto,' said Mum. (I hate her at this point.) 'Why don't you sit down for a glass of wine. Your uncle is just about finished feeding the cows. I am sure he'd like to see you, too.'

'Thank you,' said Berto, and poured himself a glass of wine. With the glass in his hand he advanced towards the stove.

'What have you cooked today, aunt?' he asked, pushing his already long nose towards the top of the stove, pretending to be natural. 'Oh, I see, oyster mushrooms. How lucky. Bet you won't tell me where you found them, Stefano. Secret place, eh?'

And before I knew it the bugger grabed some bread from the table and started scooping mushrooms into his large gob, directly from the pot, the rude man. I can see him doing it, with the tip of his nose going shiny from the oil, talking about the bloody opera he had seen the night before, drinking to help push down the food quickly.

He ate the lot.

Mum said nothing. She knew.

I was thinking about noses: that Pinocchio's grew with lies, and this other Pinocchio who had stuck his nose into the pot.

I did not visit that side of the family for at least twelve months.

CRESPELLE DI RICOTTA E FUNGHI
CREPES WITH RICOTTA AND MUSHROOMS

Crêpes are a very old-fashioned Italian food but good value, fairly easy to prepare and to prepare ahead of time. We are all used to crêpes as desserts, but perhaps a little less as a savoury food. Italians go crazy for them with various delicate fillings and I am no exception. They are great comfort food.

Serves 10 comfortably

PREPARATION TIME: 2 HOURS
COOKING TIME: 15 MINUTES

500 mL (2 cups) milk
5 eggs
¾ cup plain (all-purpose) flour
a pinch of salt
olive oil

FILLING

4 cups sliced mushrooms
4 tablespoons butter
2 cloves garlic, finely chopped
400 g (13 oz) ricotta cheese
1 egg
1 cup grated parmesan cheese
a touch of grated nutmeg
salt and pepper

500 mL (2 cups) Béchamel Sauce
(see page 100)

For the crêpes, combine all the ingredients (except the oil) little by little in a bowl and set aside for a couple of hours.

Heat a little olive oil in a frypan and swirl to coat the surface. Add about a tablespoon of batter and swirl a little to spread. Cook until set on one side. Flip crêpe with the aid of an egg-lifter and cook and lightly brown on the other side. Remove and set aside. Repeat the procedure until all the batter has been used up. Make sure the crêpes are evenly cooked, thin and soft — I like to think of them as *frittatine*, thin frittatas.

For the filling, cook the mushrooms in butter and a touch of garlic to end up with one cup. Reduce to a pulp in a food processor. Mix with the ricotta, egg, parmesan cheese, nutmeg, and salt and pepper to taste.

To assemble the dish: place a crêpe on a workbench and spoon ½ cup of filling on the top left quarter of the crêpe above the middle line. Fold the bottom half up over the filling and then the right side over that. You will be left with a triangular shape, one side of which has three overlapping layers.

Spread the béchamel sauce over the bottom of a large baking dish and arrange the crêpes with the three-layered side down. The top side will only have one layer of crêpe and will cook to a golden colour. You can spread some béchamel sauce over the crêpes if you wish

Bake in an oven preheated to 180°C (350°F) for about 15 minutes. Cover the tray with foil for the first 10 minutes or so.

CRESPELLE AGLI ASPARAGI
CREPES WITH ASPARAGUS

Once you have mastered the simple skill of crêpe-making, you can vary the fillings. One of my favourites is cream of asparagus, which must be held together by some ricotta cheese. Surprisingly, the ricotta content will be submerged by the flavour of the asparagus. Do make sure the asparagus is well creamed, for there is nothing worse than stringy bits!

Serves 10

PREPARATION TIME: 2 HOURS

COOKING TIME: 15 MINUTES

1 quantity of crêpe batter (see page 135)

ASPARAGUS CREAM

1 onion, finely chopped

olive oil

1 kg (2 lb) fresh asparagus, trimmed and chopped

knob of butter

500 mL (2 cups) chicken stock or water

salt and pepper

FILLING

1 quantity Asparagus Cream (see above)

500 g (1 lb) ricotta cheese

1/2 cup grated parmesan cheese

2 eggs

500 mL (2 cups) Béchamel Sauce (see page 100) — make the béchamel lighter by adding more milk or reducing the flour content

Prepare the crêpes as set out on page 135. Set aside until ready to use.

To make the asparagus cream: fry the onion gently in a little oil in a frypan. When ready, put the onion, asparagus, butter, water or stock, and salt and pepper in a pot. Cover with a lid and cook until the asparagus is soft. Discard the stalky bits and run the mixture through a mouli or food processor until smooth. Cool.

Make the crêpe filling by combining the ricotta, parmesan cheese, eggs and asparagus cream.

To assemble the dish: place a crêpe on a workbench and spoon 1/2 cup of filling on the top left quarter of the crêpe above the middle line. Fold the bottom half up over the filling and then the right side over that. You will be left with a triangular shape, one side of which has three overlapping layers.

Spread the béchamel sauce over the bottom of a large baking dish and arrange the crêpes three-layered side down and not overlapping too much. The top side will only have one layer of crêpe and will cook to a golden colour. Spread some extra béchamel sauce if you like. Sprinkle with parmesan cheese and finely diced and skinned fresh tomato for colour.

Bake in an oven preheated to 180°C (350°F) for about 15 minutes. Cover the tray with foil for the first 10 minutes or so.

CRESPELLE AL SALMONE
CREPES WITH SALMON

These crespelle are very delicate. I have served literally thousands of them because they are also an honest function food.

Serves 10

PREPARATION TIME: 2 HOURS
COOKING TIME: 15 MINUTES

1 quantity crêpes batter (see page 135)

FILLING

600 g (20 oz) salmon, free of all bones
and cut into 1 x 2 cm (¼ x ½ inch pieces)

24 whole basil leaves

2 cups diced ripe tomato

1 cup grated parmesan cheese

salt and pepper

500 mL (2 cups) cream

500 mL (2 cups) Béchamel Sauce
(see page 100) — make the sauce lighter by
using fish or chicken stock instead of milk

Prepare and cook the crêpes as instructed on page 135.

To assemble the dish, place a crêpe on a workbench then put 3 to 4 pieces of salmon in the top left quarter of the crêpe above the middle line. Follow with a basil leaf, a spoonful each of tomato and parmesan cheese, and sprinkle with salt and pepper. Fold the bottom half up over the filling and then the right side over that. You will be left with a triangular shape, one side of which has three overlapping layers.

Spread the bottom of a baking dish with the light béchamel sauce. When the crêpes bake they have the capacity to absorb a fair bit of sauce. If you cannot be bothered making a béchamel sauce, use the cream instead. It is not the same, but it will do, especially if you mix the cream with more diced tomato, extra parmesan cheese, salt and pepper.

Place the crêpes in the dish in barely overlapping order. Bake for approximately 15 minutes in an oven preheated to 180°C (350°F) until a nice crust forms on top, but no more otherwise the filling will dry out.

PIATTI FORTI

STRONG COURSES WITH VEGETABLES AND STORIES

I feel compelled to share some thoughts of the subject of main courses, or strong dishes as I like to call them. Mind you, not that they are always 'forti': it is that they usually require a higher level of skill or commitment. It seems to me, from an Australian perspective, that there is too much of a preconceived idea here about what is supposed to be an Italian main course. *Osso buco* comes to mind, in consort with a myriad of *veal scaloppine*, the odd grilled fish, the odd chicken breast (more international than Italian), a *costata di manzo* here and there which will never be like the famous Florentine steak, but is probably as good as meat is in Australia, depending on the capability of the cook. Of late there has been a great deal of veal shank, veal chops and other bits of veal, mostly by creative Australian chefs who must find it challenging — as I do — to present Italian main courses that are not in the usual range expected by the popular palate.

Italian cuisine is a lot more than what we are accustomed to in Australia, perhaps even a lot more than what contemporary Italians are used to. A lot of it has to do with produce, or the lack of it, or with a different emphasis on the same produce. For example, from central to southern Italy you could say that lamb is a pillar in gastronomic terms as it is in Australia. Yet most Italians would cook their lamb as *abbacchio*, which is really milk-fed and young lamb, something that Australians find a turn-off.

You will also find that each part of an animal is accorded its place and status, whether it comes from the extremities, inside or outside. The *coratella*, the quickly fried liver, lung and heart of lamb or veal, is a dish that would attract very few supporters here in Australia, yet would be eaten in Rome as a matter of fact.

The fact is that Italians cannot afford meat like the Australians think they do, and so they learnt to eat everything and to make delicious recipes out of everything. Once I cooked a piece of chuck for some friends who are meat producers; extracted a terrific *jus*, made some feather-light gnocchi; dressed them with the *jus* and good parmesan cheese. They hated the gnocchi, but they didn't mind the meat, which, for me, had become a secondary dish. Later, in conversation, I discovered that they fight for the milk gut when they slaughter an animal. I wouldn't have imagined these people ate the milk gut, again a great delicacy I enjoy when in Rome. (I also braised some ox tongue which they could not bring themselves to taste!)

I have also harped on the versatility of pork. In Australia it has been reduced to a lean meat of little consequence. A good pork roast is one of the great dishes of Italian cooking, yet rarely will you find it in Italian restaurants in Australia. It is as if pork was only good for a pub roast.

The sea surrounds Italy. Much of its cuisine is fish based. Fish lovers in Australia can easily marry Italian flavours to local fish and crustaceans. I think Australia probably possesses all the elements to make a proper fish soup, or *caciucco*, unlike other countries in the world outside the Mediterranean. This is one of the territories still quite unexplored, and I have tried to cover a little of the ground in this book.

Italians are crazy about birds and other game. There has been much development in Australia in the quest to produce birds of consistent quality and quantity. I think there is still a long way to go before the public at large can experiment with game without disappointment, or pay $8 for a squab of some quality. New products, from possum to kangaroo, ostrich to crocodile, camel to goat are becoming more available. It will be interesting to see if one can use these products and teach them 'Italian'. I have tasted some kind of air-dried ostrich as good as *bresaola* — Mildura-farmed ostrich, I must add.

The recent availability of free-range or corn-fed chickens has enabled us to return this bird to the table and to a position of prestige where it has always belonged prior to mass production. I feel so comfortable serving chicken these days and look at ways of making it appear more and more, from cold to hot dishes — poached, roasted and so on. If you really want to get into the spirit of Italian cooking get on to your chooks and play to your heart's content! Ducks, too, are better than ever and there is opportunity for the astute Italophile to exploit some great recipes.

For me main courses are as important as the *antipasti* and the *primi*: the very idea of main course is contradictory because we hardly get there. I guess it would be better to stop calling them mains. I call it a *piatto forte* and serve a smaller quantity.

The pleasure of cooking Italian is that I can present many dishes that are part of my stock of peasant memories: some are part of the 'tradition' of perceived Italian food; some can be elevated to the status of international cuisine, requiring finesse and a concentration of flavours; some use peculiarly Australian ingredients; and some can blend East and West simply because I cannot go to a market in modern Australia with blinkers on.

I have listed all these possibilities to encourage you to explore, to throw in a little ginger here and there, a sprig of coriander or a pinch of garam masala simply because we are young and free. By using the vast resources of old Italian cuisine and adding a little of the new we'll go to incredible places of the imagination and the senses.

Pollo all'Aceto
Chicken with Red Vinegar

I imagine this to be an uncomplicated chicken dish to be served with salad on a sunny day.

Serves 4

PREPARATION TIME: 10 MINUTES
COOKING TIME: 30 MINUTES

1 onion, finely chopped

3 cloves garlic, chopped

4 tablespoons good olive oil

a knob of butter

1 x 1.7 kg (3 ¼ lb) free-range chicken, cut into small pieces and dusted lightly with flour

salt and pepper

2 bay leaves

60 mL (¼ cup) good-quality red-wine vinegar (not balsamic)

4 anchovy fillets

Fry the onion and garlic in oil and butter until golden. Add the chicken and fry on all sides. Season lightly and add the bay leaves. Place a lid on the frying pan and let the chicken cook gently. From time to time you may have to add some water or stock.

When the chicken is nearly ready — do not overcook, please — raise the heat and throw in the vinegar and anchovies. Make sure the anchovies are well blended in and that the vinegar evaporates. Replace the lid and take the whole thing to the table. When you open the lid the smell of vinegar should hit your nostrils and stimulate the appetite.

POLLO CON PATATE, POMODORI E OLIVE
CHICKEN WITH POTATOES, TOMATOES AND OLIVES

A very primitive dish, ideal for an informal get-together, scented with rosemary.
The better the quality of the chicken, the better the result.

Serves 6–8

PREPARATION AND COOKING TIME:
1 ½ HOURS

1 cup chopped root vegetables, for example
carrot, celery, onion

3 cloves garlic, chopped

olive oil

1 x 1.7 kg (3 ¼ lb) free-range chicken,
cut into pieces

60 mL (¼ cup) white wine

6 medium-sized potatoes, peeled and
cut into chunks

salt and pepper

2 x 400 g (14 oz) cans Italian tomatoes, pulped

1 handful Ligurian or other olives

small sprig rosemary leaves

Fry the root vegetables (except the potatoes) and garlic in oil until fragrant, then brown the chicken pieces.

Add the white wine and potatoes. Season a little and add the pulped tomatoes. Place a lid on the pan and check progress now and then. You may have to add a little water.

Halfway through cooking add the olives — they are always a little salty — and rosemary leaves.

Ensure that the potatoes and chicken are progressing together: avoid uneven cooking. The finished dish has to be succulent. If the chicken is ready and the potatoes are not, remove the chook and keep it warm until the potatoes are ready.

This dish goes well with a green salad.

POLLO ALL'AGRESTO
CHICKEN IN THE OVEN WITH VERJUICE

I like Maggie Beer's verjuice. When I do not drink it with chilled water it finds its way into fish or chicken dishes like this.

Serves 4

PREPARATION: 35 MINUTES
COOKING TIME: 15 MINUTES

4 cloves garlic, finely chopped

a big knob of ginger, finely chopped

1 chilli, finely chopped

1 x 1.5 kg (3 lb) free-range chicken,
completely deboned and split into two halves

salt and pepper

olive oil

60 mL (¼ cup) verjuice

60 mL (¼ cup) cream

a knob of butter

basil or coriander for garnish

Preheat the oven to 180°C (350°F).

Place the garlic, ginger and chilli between the chicken breast and thigh and fold like a sandwich. Season with salt and pepper. In a cast-iron pan brown both sides in olive oil and place into the oven. Roast the chicken but remove it when it is still a little pink inside.

Rest the chicken for 10 minutes or more in a warm place. Add the verjuice to the pan, reduce on high heat, add the cream, reduce again and smooth-out the sauce away from the flame, with some butter.

Cut each side of chicken into four and dress with sauce. Sprinkle with basil or coriander.

Serve with roasted potatoes and a green salad.

QUAGLIE RIPIENE
STUFFED QUAILS

Coming from a region where every type of bird was eaten — to the point where I protested against hunting and used to go out at night with my brother Sergio and various nephews to set fire to hunters' huts — I have in me a taste for small birds. Sparrows, blackbirds, pigeons and many other birds whose names I'd have to look up in the dictionary, were a part of our diet.

When I told my little son that we used to eat sparrows he said one word: 'Sad!' That sums it all up, I guess.

With the first winter snow the fat sparrows would come near the house to peck on bait; the gun was always nearby. Kids used to spread some seeds on the snow, set up a heavy washing board leaning against a stick, attach a long string to the stick and hide. When the birds flew near the board to eat the seeds, the string would be swiftly pulled, the stick pulled away with the string and the heavy board would collapse on the poor birds. I think it only worked once, but that didn't stop us from trying for hours, year after year.

Buying farmed quails is much less romantic but much more efficient. In my career I have seen all kinds of recipes for quails — quails roasted until there wasn't anything left (my father's preference), plump quails smothered with hoisin sauce and roasted until juicy, quails deep-fried in the wok by the Vietnamese at Chinese New Year, and so on This is a fiddly but simple recipe and an all-time classic.

**Serves 4 (two quails per person
is a serious main course)**

PREPARATION TIME: 1 ½ HOURS

COOKING TIME: APPROXIMATELY
10 MINUTES

8 quails

1 cup mixed chopped celery, carrots
and onions

1 clove garlic, chopped

oil and butter for cooking

2 cups cubed chicken meat (not breast)

½ cup grated parmesan cheese

2 eggs

½ cup breadcrumbs from good bread

salt and pepper

8 thin slices pancetta or prosciutto

8 fresh sage leaves and more for the pan

extra oil and butter

125 mL (½ cup) white wine

500 mL (2 cups) smooth Tomato Sauce
(see page 37)

To bone the quails, run a sharp knife on either side of the breast bone until you expose the whole cage. Use your fingers from then on since the bones pull away rather easily. Small scissors will assist.

Gently fry the vegetables and garlic in a little oil and butter until they are soft. Add the chicken meat and cook, tossing to incorporate but not necessarily until done. Let it cool. Place the mixture in a food processor and blend. Place blended mixture in a bowl and add the parmesan cheese, eggs and breadcrumbs. You can add extra herbs if you like. Season with salt and pepper.

Preheat the oven to 180°C (350°F).

Spread the quails and place a slice of pancetta over them and a leaf of sage. Place a dollop of stuffing and roll up. Secure with a toothpick.

In a large and heavy pan sizzle butter and oil (I prefer lard). Place the quails side by side and cook until they take some colour. Turn over and colour the other side. Add some extra sage. Deglaze with white wine. Add the tomato sauce and season lightly. Place the whole thing in the oven. Bake until ready — not much more than 10 minutes — and if drying out add a little stock or water.

Saltimbocca di Quaglia
Quail Saltimbocca

Saltimbocca is usually prepared with a thin slice of veal with a thin slice of prosciutto.
The quail dish here is much the same — it will take just a little longer to cook.

Serves 4

PREPARATION TIME: 30 MINUTES
COOKING TIME: 10 MINUTES

4 plump quails

4 thin slices prosciutto

4 sage leaves

2 tablespoons butter

2 tablespoons oil

a little chopped garlic

a little white wine

4 tablespoons cream

salt and pepper

To remove all the bones from the quail, place the bird back down on a board, cut the breast on either side of the cage to expose all the bones and take it from there. Clip the wings as there is no meat on them. When the bones are removed place a slice of prosciutto and a sage leaf inside the boned bird and close it like a sandwich. Secure the ends with a toothpick. Repeat with the remaining quails.

Preheat the oven to 180°C (350°F).

Heat the butter and oil in a skillet with a metal handle and briskly seal the quails. Add a little garlic and white wine, season, and place the whole thing in the oven. Leave to cook through for 5 minutes.

Bring the skillet out, remove the quails and deglaze with a little extra white wine, season, or stock if you have some about. Reduce, add the cream and reduce again to a nice, sticky consistency.

ANITRA 'IN TECIA'

DUCK BRAISED IN SMALL PIECES

In a climate where duck now comes in a myriad of wonderful Oriental guises I am hesitant to give this recipe from a Veneto farm. I have tested it many times and it is quite passable. Of course, the thing about memories is that everything used to taste better even when it was not. With duck, though, I am sure that the farmers had a breed called the mute duck which didn't make any noise. It just emitted a strong breathing sound. What had they done to it to make it so tender and plump?

Serves 4

PREPARATION TIME: 2 HOURS
COOKING TIME: 30 MINUTES

2 cups diced root vegetables, for example carrot, celery, onion

a little olive oil

1 duck, cut into small pieces (breast in four, leg in two, etc.) and excess fat removed

a handful of sage leaves

sprig of rosemary

125 mL (½ cup) red wine

2 tablespoons tomato paste

Fry the vegetables in a little oil and add the duck pieces. Let them colour evenly, then add the sage, rosemary, wine and tomato paste. The cooking should proceed on a slow heat and the duck pieces must be accommodated side by side, not on top of each other.

Keep moist by adding hot water or stock from time to time. The duck will slowly release the fat which will merge with the vegetables. (I have not given it here, but the oldies used to put strips of lard in this dish. I do it that way and I like the juices at the end of cooking as a condiment for rigatoni, the commercial pasta.)

This dish is best accompanied by braised vegetables or by a salad.

Cotechino e Zampone
COTECHINO AND ZAMPONE

Ther is no reason why you cannot make these two pork products. All you need is the correct ingredients, the correct amount of salt, and a good butcher. Behind good food there is always a good supplier.

Cotechino is made with a good proportion – at least 30 per cent – of pork skin, very clean and finely ground. The remainder of the meat mixture is ground pork from the front of the animal with at least 30 per cent fat content. In other words, between pork skin and other fat you should end up with a total of just over 50 per cent fat. This mixture is piped into suitable casings and after a short rest period is boiled for at least two hours. A considerable amount of fat will ooze out into the cooking water. You will not be eating fat, but a very moist, textured sausage that is suitable for many uses.

Zampone refers to the section from the trotter to above the knee – practically the whole front leg. It can be (patiently) tunnelled-boned with a sharp knife and filled with the same content as the cotechino and the meat of the same leg. The skin forms the container for this sausage, which is wrapped in aluminium foil and poached just like a cotechino. After the foil is discarded you are left with a soft, stuffed leg which cuts into pretty slices. It can be difficult to obtain a section of the leg which has not been already cut up into hocks and trotters. A good butcher should be able to assist.

For cotechino and *zampone* I will not give precise quantities as how much you make is up to you. What you need for cotechino is CLEAN skin (from the butcher) for standard salami, string and one of those old-fashioned machines that pipe the farce into the skin. The ratio for 1 kg minced (ground) pork (skins and meat) is 30 g (2 ½ tablespoons) salt and 5g (1 teaspoon) coarse black pepper. It is important to work the mince and the condiments for quite some time, 'kneading' it with your hands so that the salt and pepper are evenly distributed. It is equally important not to go over these measurements or the final product may be too salty or peppery.

After you have stuffed the skin, tie each end with string, prick the sausage all over lightly. This cotechino can be boiled immediately, but will keep for several weeks in the coolest part of the refrigerator.

Zampone requires the same stuffing and, depending on the size of the leg, you may have to cook it for two to three hours at a gentle simmer wrapped in foil.

Both dishes go with the condiments of *bollito misto*, lentils or peas or potatoes and any number of steamed vegetables.

Spezzatino di Pancetta alla Maniera di Tony

PORK BELLY IN SOY AND GARLIC

My friend the chef Tony Tan knows how fond I am of pork. One evening at his house he presented me with a dish of stewed pork belly that is popular among the Chinese communities in the Malacca Straits and in Penang. He accompanied it with wok-fried swamp cabbage — kangkong, quite spiced — and I thought it was fantastic.

Serves 4 or more
COOKING TIMES: 2 HOURS OR MORE UNTIL
THE PORK IS SO TENDER IT FALLS APART

1–2 tablespoons peanut oil

7 cloves garlic, crushed and skins on

4 teaspoons sugar

salt and freshly ground black pepper

600 g (1 ¼ lb) pork belly, cut into
2 cm (³/₄ inch) square cubes

2 teaspoons light soy sauce

1 teaspoon dark soy sauce

750 mL (3 cups) water

In a saucepan, heat the oil and fry the garlic cloves until lightly golden. Add the sugar, salt, pepper and pork. Fry the sugar a little and let it caramelise so it coats the meat with a glaze in the process.

Add the soy sauces and continue to fry another minute or so. Pour in the water and stir gently until the soy sauces dissolve. Bring to the boil, and skim any impurities that rise to the surface. Cover and simmer for about 2 hours, until the meat is tender and the sauce is syrupy.

Arrosto di Pancetta

SLOW-ROASTED PORK BELLY

*The belly has to cook very slowly and you will see it rising in height, almost as if you had injected it with yeast.
It is a beautiful thing to see — little wonder why the Chinese call the meat something like 'five-flowered pork'.*

Serves 8

PREPARATION TIME: 5 MINUTES
COOKING TIME: 5 HOURS' SLOW BAKING

2 kg (4 lb) belly pork, ribs removed
250 mL (1 cup) water
1 knob ginger, chopped very coarsely
6 cloves garlic, chopped very coarsely

Preheat the oven to 110–120°C (200–250°F).

Wash the belly. Place it in a heavy baking dish, skin down, pour in the water, sprinkle generously with ginger and garlic, cover with aluminium foil, and place in the oven. Check after 1 hour to see that the temperature is not so low that nothing is happening and not so high that too much heat is going in too quickly.

After about 5 hours the meat will melt in the mouth. The skin, though, can be as hard as a rock. Peel off the skin with the aid of a knife or a spatula. This meat will be tender because it has cooked between natural layers of fat which have melted in the cooking.

Serve with a salad of thinly sliced cabbage dressed with a good-quality balsamic vinegar.

Note: You can smear the belly before cooking with *char siu* sauce for a Chinese taste.

Arrosto di Maiale con il Finocchio Selvaggio

LEG OF PORK STUFFED WITH WILD FENNEL

Wild fennel is a versatile herb with a strong aroma. Its strong flavour unites with garlic to combat the often-unappealing smell of roasted pork. Pig-farming in Australia has a long way to go before it delivers a product of quality — too much fat has been taken out of the meat to pander to people who worry about diets but do not exercise or work hard. Industry people should also know that the unappealing smell is not something that consumers should have to put up with. Before the consumption of pork declines even further they should take steps to rectify these problems.

Get your butcher to remove the bone from a leg of pork. Pick some wild fennel along a creek or a country road — it grows everywhere in southern Australia. Choose a location where it is unlikely that the council has sprayed herbicides!

Serves 10–12

PREPARATION TIME: 20 MINUTES
COOKING TIME: 2–3 HOURS

1 cup wild fennel flowers, better
if dried with seeds

5 cloves garlic

1 tablespoon coarse sea salt

1 leg pork, whole and bone removed

6–7 wild fennel stalks

Preheat the oven to 180° C (350° F).

Crush fennel flowers and seeds in a food processor with garlic and salt. Rub the paste inside the leg and stuff the hole with bundled up fennel stalks, as many as will fit in. It will look, of course, rather rustic with bits of stalks sticking out on each side. These are even likely to burn in the high temperatures of the oven. It does not matter and actually looks good.

Place in a baking tray and cook for 2–3 hours. Any leftovers can be sliced and used in sandwiches.

Fegato di Maiale nella Rete

PORK LIVER IN CAUL FAT

I have to give you this recipe even if you end up thinking that all I cook is pork! If you are not keen on liver, move on, but I must remind readers that Italian cooking is more than veal scaloppine and that the secondi piatti are often a consequence of the first course (a salad of meat after you have made the stock, for instance) or offal delicacies like this.

Serves 4

PREPARATION TIME: 10 MINUTES
(AFTER SOAKING)

12 pieces pork caul fat, approximately
8 x 8 cm (3 x 3 inches)

12 slices pork liver, thinly sliced

12 sage leaves

salt and pepper

6 tablespoons olive oil

balsamic vinegar, to taste

A good butcher should give you a small quantity of pork caul fat that is white like snow. If reddish, keep washing in cold water and soak for several hours. Slice pork liver to 4 mm (¼ inch) thickness.

Cut a square of caul, place a slice of liver and top with a sage leaf. Season with salt and pepper, fold the caul up and fry quickly in a small amount of olive oil until golden. Do not overcook liver or it goes tough, so make sure the liver is fresh when you buy it.

You can splash generously with balsamic vinegar if you like and serve with runny white polenta (see page 52).

Medaglioni di Vitello con Fontina e Spinaci Cotti

VEAL MEDALLIONS WITH FONTINA AND SPINACH TOPPING

A dish similar to scaloppine, except that you work with thicker medallions of veal and finish the dish in the oven. Veal straps are easily arranged through a good butcher. Choose a nice melting cheese like fontina, available from good delis.

Serves 4

PREPARATION TIME: 1 HOUR
COOKING TIME: 10 MINUTES

4 veal straps, cleaned and cut into three or four pieces

a little flour to coat the veal

butter and oil for frying

salt and pepper

250 mL (1 cup) cream

4 tablespoons chopped cooked spinach

a few thin slices fontina cheese

Preheat the oven to 180° C (350° F).

Place the veal pieces on a chopping board, cover with plastic and bash out into round medallions which are not too thin (like *scaloppine*) or too thick (like steak). Lightly flour the veal.

Heat a pan with a metal handle (it will be shoved into the oven), add butter and oil and as soon as it sizzles add the medallions. Brown them on both sides, season, and continue cooking until you see the blood droplets oozing out.

Add the cream, lower the heat and, working fast, place a tablespoon or spinach on each medallion and a slice of cheese. Place into the oven to melt cheese for 4–5 minutes.

Pastissada di Collo di Manzo
POT-ROASTED CHUCK

Serves 6–8

COOKING TIME: 4–5 HOURS

10 cloves garlic, slivered

2 kg (4 lb) piece chuck, that is, meat
from the neck

½ cup mixed rosemary and sage leaves

olive oil

1 onion, chopped

500 mL (2 cups) robust red wine

750 mL (3 cups) chicken or beef
stock or water

Tomato Sauce (see page 37), optional

Stick the garlic into the meat here and there and season with the herbs. Tie up with a piece of string. Heat a small amount of olive oil in a heavy-bottomed pot and brown the meat. Add the onion, cook until translucent, then add the wine. Stir, then add the stock and braise on low heat for several hours with the lid on. Turn the meat from time to time. When cooked, it must fall apart. Make sure it does not dry out or you won't have the necessary tasty sauce.

About two hours before the *pastissada* is ready you have the option of adding some tomato sauce. If you do, the resulting sauce will be excellent with pasta. I dare say that most of the time I prepare this dish for the sauce rather than the meat!

SPEZZATINO DI CARNE

ITALIAN-STYLE BEEF STEW

Stews are old fashioned and I love them. They are easy and liberated, a kind of cooking in shorts. They are almost universal, non-political, non-trendy and generous to a fault. Why ignore them? Potatoes work well as thickening agents.

In some pubs run by Italian families you can still find a good spezzatino. *The Clare Castle Hotel in Carlton (Melbourne) was, and still is, a place where Italian men would gather at lunch, especially in the winter, for a bowl of* spezzatino.

Serves 6

PREPARATION TIME: 3 HOURS,
MOSTLY COOKING TIME

2 largish carrots, roughly chopped

2 onions, roughly chopped

2 stalks celery, roughly chopped

olive oil

2 cloves garlic, left whole

1.5 kg (3 lb) stewing meat (beef or amb),
cut into rough cubes

250 mL (1 cup) red wine

5 medium-sized potatoes, cubed

500 g (1 lb) crushed, peeled tomatoes

1 small bay leaf

salt and pepper

Cook the carrots, onions and celery in olive oil until a little brown. Add the garlic towards the end so it doesn't burn. Add the meat, seal it and pour in the red wine. When it has evaporated add the potatoes and tomatoes, bay leaf and some salt and pepper.

Stew on gentle heat for 2 hours or more, with the lid partly on. The potatoes will break down and so will the meat in due course. You may have to add a little water or stock as you go.

A *spezzatino* goes well with a salad of red radicchio. I like the vinegar flavour of the dressing and the bitterness of radicchio with the flavour of the stew.

Animelle con i Carciofi
LAMB SWEETBREADS WITH ARTICHOKES

Lamb sweetbreads are delicious. The Italians consider them a rarity and are more accustomed to the larger sweetbreads from veal. In Australia we are more likely to find excellent sweetbreads because of the abundance of lambs.

For this recipe you need very good, tender artichokes. If artichokes are not available, use green asparagus or spinach.

Serves 4

PREPARATION TIME: 1 HOUR 20 MINUTES
COOKING TIME: 10 MINUTES

500 g (1 lb) prepared sweetbreads

5 tender artichokes (outer leaves and chokes removed) (see page 112 for preparation method)

butter

salt and pepper

extra butter

3 slices fatty pancetta or prosciutto, cut into matchsticks

60 mL (¼ cup) white wine

To clean the *animelle* (this means 'little souls'), soak them in cold water until all blood — if there is any — has been removed. Cover with cold water and bring to the boil for 1 minute. Cool and peel all membranes, bits of fat or sinew. The sweetbreads are now ready for use.

Slice the artichokes thinly and fry gently in butter. Season with salt and pepper and put aside. Heat some butter and toss the sweetbreads for a couple of minutes or less — they are already cooked. Remove the *animelle*, fry the prosciutto in the same pan and deglaze with wine.

Place the *animelle* on a platter surrounded by the artichokes and pour the contents of the frying pan over them.

Brasato di Lingua di Bue
Braised Ox Tongue with Star Anise

Italians eat all these strange things and don't even blink. I have said elsewhere that the use of offal is what makes Italian cooking something special. We only know a fraction of the offal dishes that are part of the repertoire of Italian cooking. In Australia we are so used to veal scaloppine *and chicken* parmigiana — *a dish that actually does not exist in Italy — that we happily ignore all those bits and pieces that have provided pleasure for centuries and that actually define the character of a national cuisine.*

Here braised tongue is teamed with star anise, that beautiful aromatic spice from Asia.

Serves 4–6
COOKING TIME: 3 HOURS, BUT WITH
LITTLE ATTENTION TO THE POT

I tongue, simmered for I hour

6 lardons (strips of pork fat from the belly),
4 cm (1 1/2 inch) long and the thickness
of a pencil

I small onion, chopped into small dice

I small carrot, chopped into small dice

I stalk celery, chopped into small dice

2 cloves garlic, chopped

olive oil

2 pieces pork skin from the belly, 10 cm x 5 cm
(4 x 2 inches) or thereabouts (optional)

250 mL (I cup) red wine

I L (4 cups) chicken or beef stock

2 cloves

3 star anise

Strip the partly cooked tongue of its membrane. Cut six holes at random and insert the lardons (a round and pointed object will help).

In a heavy-based pan sauté the onion, carrot, celery and garlic in a little oil and the pork skin, if using, until they are soft. Add the tongue and the red wine. Cook gently until the wine is almost gone. Add the cloves.

Add the stock, cover with a lid and cook gently for 2 hours, turning the tongue from time to time. Do not let the tongue dry out. Add water if you have to.

When it is soft — and the pork skin is so soft you can eat it with a spoon — remove the pot from the fire and add the star anise: the spice will infuse the sauce with its exotic aroma without actually overpowering it. As the tongue is resting skim the fat as it rises to the top. Do this well and systematically and you will not need to chill the sauce. This dish can be made ahead in which case the fat will set in the fridge. Skim off before reheating gently.

This is a dish best enjoyed with polenta but also goes well with steamed rice or a white risotto (see page 93), a plain risotto made with stock and cheese.

THE GRAN BOLLITO MISTO

If there is one thing that sends shivers down my back, it is the memory of the bollito misto trolley which is often found in northern Italian restaurants. The bollito misto is, in a way, the grandest of all dishes, the most decadent, and the most difficult — I must confess — to sell to both my friends and customers. I have concluded that the bollito misto must be an attitude, a state of mind, or a cultural predisposition.

To help you understand what the bollito is, I will put it in context for you. "Bollito' is the Italian past participle for 'boiled'. As often with past participles, an article in front turns them into nouns. So, bollito becomes the word for a selection of meats that has been boiled or, more technically speaking, poached.

Now assume it is a cold day out there, so you order a bowl of soup made with one of the stocks which has been produced by one of the bollito parts, for example, chicken or beef or a blend of both. The soup may be plain or contain some tortellini. In winter this is a very special treat designed to warm you up and to prepare the stomach for what is to come.

Then you have the bollito itself, or parts thereof: these are the meats that have been boiled such as capon or chicken; beef sheen or any other beef part with a fat component; ox tongue; cotechino or zampone.

Cotechino and zampone (see page 150) are boiled for a long time to break down the fat and to create that special stickiness which is what makes these two meats so attractive.

Pickles, sauces and vegetables play a key role in this dish. Cotechino or zampone requires a strong stimulant like freshly grated horseradish dressed with vinegar; pink and tender ox tongue looks good next to a green sauce made with parsley, capers and eggs; beef can do with any mustard, especially quince mustard, although a garlic mayonnaise is also very good.

Vegetables such as carrots, celery and onions are slowly cooked in one of the stocks, and cooked they must be — there is no room here for crunchy vegetables. They can be kept moist in a suitable platter, covered with hot stock and a drizzle of good olive oil. Mashed potatoes are compulsory, although boiled potatoes dressed with oil and parsley are also very good. Gherkins, giardiniera, preserved pickles like capsicums (bell peppers) in vinegar, eggplants (aubergines) in oil, and so on are all compatible with a bollito.

One does not have to eat all these combinations, especially for lunch! I have shown you the full picture because it is so fascinating. Think of a steaming trolley containing most of these things. Imagine a cold and rainy day outside… there is some sawdust at the entrance of the restaurant and as people enter they are shaking off the rain, or removing warm overcoats. The restaurant itself is warm and comfortable, a little old-fashioned, but accessible to all the workers in the neighbourhood — you can read the newspaper if you are by yourself before you order. Mezzo litro della casa, cameriere, *and* acqua minerale. *Perhaps I am just an incurable romantic and these restaurants exist only in my imagination, though I remember them clearly from when I was a kid. Melbourne is the ideal city for a* gran bollito misto *on a Sunday, especially during the colder months — it's a kind of Italian answer to* yum cha.*

I have to say that a whole generation of past restaurateurs, perhaps from southern Italy where the bollito misto *does not play a main role, let this chance go. The young ones have become victims of what I call smart food — a* bruschetta e via, *a lump of cheese and a glass of wine, and see you later. Spunky surroundings with close little tables, cute little lamps, lots of logos, lots of board menus and cute people sipping* lattè — *pronounced 'lattay' — everywhere. This had to happen in Melbourne as a reaction to too much wowserism, to no sense of hospitality, to restaurants hidden away for a furtive elite (I always had the impression that The Latin before Bill Marchetti took over was underground!) or, like the Waiters Club (another Melbourne establishment), only for those initiated to the mysteries of a chipped cup of rough red. And to pubs, smelly pubs everywhere, divided into saloons and ladies lounges, as if demanding a little cleanliness made one less of a man.*

For a cup of espresso you had to travel miles, to machines that were never cleaned, to coffee that was stale or burnt. All of this is now gone, and our cities are much better for it. But the Italian community, while remaining a driving force, or just being the driving force in some areas, has not imposed a cuisine consistent with its glorious tradition. We simply do not have a string of regional restaurants presenting the array of dishes that, say, the Chinese are able to show us today. The fact that the gran bollito misto *never entered the Italo-Australian cuisine idiom and perhaps never will is just an example of this vacuum. You were more likely to find a* bollito — *or parts of it — at the old Stephanie's Restaurant in Hawthorn than at any Italian restaurants. She had taken the trouble to understand it, an effort young Italo-Australian chefs do not seem culturally equipped to undertake. It takes a lot more than designer food to create, sustain and develop further Italian food in Australia.*

A bollito *is not a recipe in precise quantities. Do it in largish quantities and invite your best friends to Sunday lunch.*

Simmer 1 fat and plump capon or chicken in a pot of cold water with all the necessary vegetables for a good stock and a pinch of salt.

Put 2 ox tongues, preferably those that have been in brine for a few days, in a pot with water and various root vegetables and a large tablespoon of allspice and bring to a simmer.

Put 2 kg of an inferior cut of beef, preferably with some fat attached, in a pot with hot water and various root vegetables and a pinch of salt.

Put 1 large cotechino, skin pierced in a few spots with the tip of a sharp knife, wrapped in clean cloth or aluminium foil to prevent it from breaking, in a pot covered with cold water.

Now start simmering everything. You are the conductor and all these pots are your orchestra. Skim the fat, keep the meats submerged in liquid, turn down the flame if need be.

In the meantime prepare your vegetables. Make nice batons out of carrots, cut the leeks into quarters, select young onions or small onions to be poached with the other two vegetables.

Place potatoes in a pot ready for mash, or you can leave them whole, especially if you have small ones.

Prepare your *salsa verde*. Here is my recipe:

4 hard-boiled eggs
1 clove garlic
5 anchovy fillets
1 tablespoon small capers in vinegar
2 small potatoes, boiled
salt
2 packed cups Italian (flat-leaf) parsley, very finely chopped
olive oil to bind
lemon juice for extra acid

Mash all ingredients in the food processor, except the parsley, oil and lemon juice. Add parsley to the food processor. Whiz, adding a little oil and lemon juice. A few seconds will bring all ingredients together in a nice green sauce with a certain piquancy. A little salt may be required as the anchovies may not be salty enough. This sauce is good for the tongue but also for the other parts of the bollito, especially the chicken.

I now assume that at least one pot can be turned off. This will be the chicken. Let it sit there. The next one to come off will be the beef: note — this must be soft and tender. Now you have two pots and two stocks.

Taste them, and in mid-morning a nice cup of hot stock may be just what you need.

Take out equal amounts of beef and chicken stock for your soup. You may reduce this to concentrate flavours. Another quantity of half-and-half stock can be placed in a very shallow and large saucepan. Here you will place side by side all the prepared vegetables and you will begin to cook them, for they do take a while to soften.

Hopefully the tongues are coming along, but it doesn't matter if they are not: they can keep on cooking during pre-lunch drinks and even during all the other preliminaries. So can the cotechino, although it is likely to be ready. It can rest happily in its pot. So can the potatoes if they have the skins on. If you mash them, do it ahead of your guests arriving and keep the mash in a very low oven in a suitable vessel. Remember that mashing potatoes is an art. Choose appropriate potatoes and put them through the finest holes of your mouli. Plenty of butter or olive oil or both are necessary for flavour, and for a creamy texture, why not a little bit of cream? Don't forget salt, like most people do. Your arteries will harden only if you sit on your bum all day.

Now organise all your other sauces: if you find some natural horseradish, peel and grate it. Pour some white vinegar over it. Place in bowl all the bits and pieces you like: mustards, French and English, *mostarda Veneta* (a confection of quince and an assortment of cute small fruits looking like a dense jam and flavoured with mustard — available from specialist Italian stores, from very mild to quite hot), little black olives, etc.

After all the preliminaries of your choice, sit your guests down. Serve them a bowl of broth, with or without tortellini (if you can make these all the better; some commercial ones are fine) as long as there is plenty of *Grana Padano* cheese in it and it is available on the table.

Then proceed with the bollito proper. Have ready a very large platter. Place some stock on the bottom to warm it. Pull off the breasts and legs of the chicken, slice some beef and cotechino. Remove the outer skin of the tongue and slice the tongue as well. Place everything on the platter and pour more stock over the top. The stock will keep things hot and moist. In a separate platter organise your vegetables: potatoes in the centre, all others around. Sprinkle with good salt. Pour some gorgeous olive oil over the lot and, again, some stock.

Take both platters to the table and eat without further ado. A fennel or radicchio salad or both would be very appropriate at this stage. You may well ask what is the pleasure of eating boiled meats. To begin they are all different in flavour and, especially, in texture. Then you have the sauces to complement the meats: these can be very interesting. Green, French, English, horseradish all add more dimensions. As I said, I admit that it is difficult to persuade people that this is more than a glorified dish of corned beef. But *bollito misto* is more, and I'll leave it at that.

PIATTI FORTI

WINTER: THE APOGEE OF RADICCHIO

If you think that radicchio (*rosso*) is just a reddish, bitter lettuce, another addition to your salad, but not an indispensable one, you are underestimating it. It is likely that radicchio does not feature at all in your culinary panorama or that, at best, you know little about it, a situation caused, among other reasons and in my opinion, by the excessive bitterness of the vegetable in Australia. It is a pity that the public has not been given a real opportunity to savour the full range of radicchios.

There are many types of red radicchio and even more green ones, though I have rarely seen green radicchio in Australian shops, even though many Italians and other migrants grow green radicchio at home.

Red radicchio is usually associated with the Veneto region, and comes in various forms: radicchio di Castelfranco, radicchio di Chioggia and radicchio di Treviso, each referring to the three provincial centres in the Veneto. There is a fourth type, a derivation of the Treviso variety, called radicchio di Verona, yet another Veneto town, which was created through horticultural seed selection in the 1950s. The latter variety exists in Australia.

The first variety looks like a large rose with tender leaves in white, light green and specks of red. Castelfranco, by the way, is a beautiful medieval township between Treviso and Vicenza. It was the place of birth of Giorgione, that painter of many enigmatic pictures, including 'The Tempest', which must be the most mysterious of all his works and perhaps the most puzzling work of the Italian Renaissance. The radicchio di Castelfranco — the Castellano — is a cross-breeding of radicchio di Treviso with a type of endive late last century.

A better one for me is the radicchio di Chioggia, grown in the sandy soils of orchards near Venice's little sister. This was derived from the Castelfranco radicchio in the 1930s. It is crunchier and tighter than, say, the Castellano. For these reasons it is a good pickling radicchio, sometimes found in specialist shops here in Australia, especially at Melbourne's Enoteca Sileno. It is a great addition to the range of Italian *sambals* — if I can use this expression — that enhance a *bollito misto* or make an *antipasto* a little extra special. I have seen this in Australia but I cannot tell if it was grown consciously as radicchio di Chioggia.

A variety absolutely never seen in Australian shops is the radicchio di Treviso, arguably the best of all and the parent of all others. Its seeds are readily available in Australia, but I doubt people know what to do with it. This is a crunchy, bittersweet lettuce, which is sometimes called *spadone* as its long leaves are somehow reminiscent of a long sword. Don't ask me why the popular imagination sees it as a sword, but then radicchio is the stuff legends are made of.

Treviso, also a lovely medieval town, has nothing to do with this horticultural triumph. It originated in the village of Dosson, five kilometres from Treviso, in the second half of last century. All the experts agree that Dosson is the epicentre of radicchio — also known as *il fiore che si mangia* (the flower that one eats). Even the local campanile — bell tower — is said to resemble the shape of the traditional tub in which radicchio used to be washed before it was sent to market. I was fortunate to be born there and by all accounts it is my family — not in an extended sense — that can lay tentative but legitimate claim to its genesis.

I hope that someone in Australia will see the potential of this versatile vegetable and initiate production. Who knows, it may, in time, displace the ubiquitous rocket (arugula)! This radicchio can be employed in salads — obviously — but it also grills and braises, especially with pancetta. Braised by itself it becomes the base of the most delicate and beautifully coloured risotto. In some ways its uses are similar to fennel, although the results are far more exotic.

The radicchio di Treviso is now grown outside the traditional boundaries of Dosson, Casier and Casale sul Sile — an area of few square kilometres — but only where the soil and the microclimate are very similar to the area of origin. In other words, where the soil is rich, free of pebbles, with more clay than sand, where the summer is warm, rainfalls are frequent and the winter rigid.

Nowadays radicchio is sown, thinned, fertilised and picked mechanically. It is ripened under controlled conditions. Long gone are the times when all these operations were conducted manually. The legends and storytelling that went on at night while preparing radicchio for the morning market have now been replaced by radicchio shows; competitions for colour, size and taste. These are held in veritable *tendopoli* — notice this Italian neologism which translates as *tentpolis*, cities of tent — under which you find entire portable professional kitchens, bars and eating facilities, armies of volunteers and armies of hungry people queuing for radicchio specialities like roasted guinea fowl and radicchio salad, braised radicchio, polenta and sausages and even radicchio cake. Chefs are encouraged to come from other parts of Italy to apply their expertise and creativity to add to the ever-expanding range of radicchio recipes.

These *festival del radicchio* invariably carry on into the night to the sound of mega-piano accordions playing tangos, lambadas, waltzes and whatever the public requests. The quantity of *grappa* downed on these occasions would cause a police state of emergency if they were transported to Australia!

Radicchio was just hard work when I was growing up. To begin with, after sowing the seeds, the shoots had to be manually thinned and this wasn't a very pleasant job, especially under the fierce August sun. My father once promised my three older brothers — who were just kids at the time — that he would take them to Venice as a reward if they helped him to complete a whole paddock by the end of August. This was an extraordinary promise at a time when you were expected to work without incentive, and by a man who wasn't often able to take time off work. That paddock of radicchio must have been important enough to warrant such bold initiative. To Venice — only 20 kilometres away — they went and had a treat of spaghetti bolognese, somewhere at the Lido. Simple pleasures, I guess.

Later, at the end of autumn, when the fog descends upon the north, enveloping everything so that by 4 p.m. you think you are blind, the radicchio begins to wilt, to rust and to rot. Now, and as in the past, is the time when radicchio is picked. It is dug out of its wet, cold and slimy soil; now by machinery, in the past with a spade. The idea is to pull up all the roots so that several plants can be bundled up. My father used long canes from a type of willow tree to tie the bundles of radicchio.

The bundles of radicchio were massed together with the root covered with soil and the top covered with straw. Later the radicchio was taken to the stable, the cow shed. There the bundles sat upright on a bed of straw and sometimes manure. Water was once or twice sprinkled over the top. In such warm and humid conditions the roots reactivate and begin to produce those beautiful and edible red and white leaves. Radicchio at this point reaches the apogee, a height no other earthly vegetable can aspire to.

It is said that it was the de Pieris who developed the radicchio with a botanist from Belgium, who had been engaged by our landlord, Count de Reali, to organise an English-style park for his villa in Dosson. It is more than likely that the botanist Francesco Van den Borre (this is how his name has been Italianised) knew the Belgian technique for whitening lettuces such as witlof, which is also in the chicory family.

Not a bad idea transforming wild chicory into an edible vegetable in a country where the only offerings in the winter were cabbages, cardoons and turnips. In those days people suffered pellagra, a dreadful condition resulting mostly from a poor diet. Pellagra was a cause of madness and in severe cases, of death. I have mentioned elsewhere the predominance of polenta in the Veneto diet up to the 1950s: last century polenta was so dominant that imbalances in the diet actually caused death. (In the four years from 1875 to 1878 there were fifty-four cases of pellagra recorded in Dosson. Of these five died.)

There is no doubt that radicchio provided a new source of much needed vitamins and of equally needed extra income for the poor farmers. I have no doubt that the health of farmers improved because of radicchio. What today would be called 'second', the produce that is not presentable at the market, was eaten at home during the winter. I am sure that the practice, typical of southern Treviso, of mixing radicchio already dressed with vinegar with pasta and fagioli as a kind of giant warm salad was a way of introducing vitamins into a standard meal, apart from being a good meal in itself. The practice of adding oil and vinegar to soups, especially *pasta e fagioli*, is probably derived from this old habit.

I am surprised that no writer — and there is a vast literature on radicchio — has explored the link between the birth of radicchio and the poverty that existed at the time. Veneto writers have unfortunately dwelt on the 'goodness' of Veneto people, on their devotion to the land and the church; they have glorified and romanticised work on the land but never paid attention to their social and economic reality.

Consumers seemed to have liked radicchio from the start because Treviso was exporting it from the turn of the century to cities like Roma and Milan in especially designed boxes and later it was flown to London, Paris and New York.

One year — this story has been told to me a million times — long before I was born, my three brothers and my father went out to dig up radicchio in the snow. As it continued to snow for some time, they were the only ones with radicchio whitening in the stable. When they took their product to the market, where other vegetables were also scarce, they made a small fortune.

Another story related to the fire that partly destroyed our original home. It is said that great-grandmother stood on her bed, flames engulfing the room, holding up high a small bag of radicchio seeds. At night our family gathered in the stable after dinner to peel the radicchio roots to make it presentable to the market. A section of the root was left on conventionally to add weight, in the same fashion that fat is left on the meat by butchers and to provide some shelf-life. But Italy was fast becoming industrial, people were leaving the land in droves and selling up their best radicchio land. Ironically, to the many factories manufacturing bricks, roof tiles and other building materials that were needed for the housing programs for peasants leaving the land.

BACCALÀ IN TWO WAYS

You have already acquainted yourself with baccalà *in antipasti (see page 40). I have such faith in* baccalà *that I would like everyone to be as excited about it as I am.*

Here are two ways of preparing cod. The first, with salted fillets, is straight-forward and easy. The second, which uses the whole dried fish, is a little more challenging, but not so fancy as to be beyond the reach of any serious 'foodie'.

Serves 6
PREPARATION TIME: EXCEPT
FOR SOAKING THE FISH, 30 MINUTES
COOKING TIME: 1 HOUR

1 kg (2 lb) salted baccalà fillets, kept
in several changes of water for 2 days

a little plain (all-purpose) flour

4 tablespoons olive oil

extra olive oil for frying

3 cloves garlic, chopped

30 small Ligurian olives, or any olives
with a low-salt taste

50 mL (⅕ cups) white wine

600 mL (2 ½ cups) Tomato Sauce
(see page 37)

THE FIRST WAY

Cut the fillets into pieces: this fish has bones that cannot be removed. Flour the cod pieces lightly and seal them in a pan in a little olive oil.

Heat the extra olive oil and fry the garlic quickly. Add the fish and olives. Add the white wine and when this has evaporated add the tomato sauce. Gently simmer for 1 hour or until soft and tasty.

Serve at once, preferably with runny polenta.

THE SECOND WAY

Here you'll need a whole dried fish. This is not salty as it has been air-dried. Soak in water for several days,
up to five days, to soften. Change the water often and to avoid unpleasant smells do it in the garage.
Dried fish is best if it is first bashed with a mallet.

Serves 5–6, depending on the size of the fish

PREPARATION TIME: 3 1/2 HOURS
COOKING TIME: 30 MINUTES

1 whole baccalà, softened and soaked
1/2 cup grated parmesan cheese
a little plain (all-purpose) flour
125 mL (1/2 cup) olive oil
3–4 onions, finely sliced
6 salted sardine fillets (fillet them under running water)
a handful of parsley
salt and freshly ground black pepper
1 L (4 cups) milk

When the fish is soft remove the skin and bones. Mix the fish with the parmesan cheese and the flour.

In a pan fry the onions in olive oil until translucent. Add the sardines and parsley.

In a small pot — preferably an earthenware pot — place a layer of onions and a layer of fish. Sprinkle with a little salt and pepper. Repeat until all ingredients are used up. Cover with milk. Cook gently — I mean gently — on the stove for 2–3 hours. Make sure that nothing sticks to the bottom. When the milk has reduced to a sauce and the *baccalà* is cooked, finish the casserole in an oven heated to 200°C (400°F) so that the top has a nice crust.

Eat hot with polenta and a rosé wine.

THE MURRAY RIVER AND ITS FISH

On the Murray, Mildura 1995

Rising from heights rare in Australia, the Murray uncoils
like a great serpent on a journey cross country, the long
line traversing, composing, all terrains — as if limming
the borders of at least three states of mind: call them the New,
the South and the Victorian. The Murray's capaciousness
is legendary, and the flow, like the great poem endless in its
variations and surety. In America, we'd
call the Murray the Mississippi, but only a blues
player and Brodsky's cat are famous for it. Rivers are
like that: you never know who they are going to invoke.
The Murray, a river of work, cutting its way through time
and all resistance: here broad and reflecting, there deep and
gorgeous in confinement — scoriated limestone valleys
of imagination — and stillness, too, in swampy
backwaters and billabongs, where the traveller, the river's
reader, can paddle about and muse on the curious
vicissitudes of Nature's Muse, who is also like a
river, only she is her own sole source of plenishment,
whereas the Murray — refreshed by loss — is both less and more.

PAUL KANE

(Written by American poet Paul Kane during his visit to the Mildura Arts Festival in 1995 and so far unpublished)

What else can one say after such eloquence? I am lucky to see the river from the window of my study. Our house is on a cliff about 20 metres above the water and the same distance from the edge. We have put up a wire mesh and temporary fence as a safety measure around the edges to stop the children from falling in: the incline is close to 90 degrees.

The light around the river is forever changing and colours my mood. Visitors come into the house and sit silently looking at the river. 'Looking at the river' is our new pastime.

The summer months bring the jet-skiing boats, which make intolerable noise and demonstrate very little respect for the natural environment.

The river is a political football — all politicians talk about it but very few governments actually do anything about it. Some change is coming from within the more progressive sectors of the farming community by way of new irrigation practices aimed at reducing salinity, but by and large the river is losing its battle for survival. I invoke ten years of experience in the public service and as an adviser to politicians to support such broad generalisations. When change happens, you see it, you feel it, it is palpable and you know where the vision is coming from. I perceive no evidence of real change here. Nearly all Mildura's stormwater, for example, flows into the river — plastic, oil, cigarette butts, bottles, you name it, in it goes — and we drink it, and South Australians drink it. And yet there are countless organisations whose brief is the river's welfare. And nothing happens. Do we need more water contamination disasters before anyone takes notice? I hope not.

The Australian poet Graeme Kinross-Smith wrote this about the Murray in his *Book of the Murray*:

In one sense, perhaps, I have seen the Murray. But in another I have hardly begun to see it. Because you can never have the Murray; it is always changing within its essential changelessness. It is always a river, but never the same river in place or time. And again, the Murray is more than a river; it is an influence, a theme, a beneficence that spreads into the country and is not above chastening it. The Murray is a hoary stream, not green banked and overhung; it is a nonchalant river, slow and powerful; a strong brown god in fact. But mere seeing is not enough. You must smell the Murray, taste it, listen to it. And soon you find you want to read its changing face wherever you can reach it, and the river is in your soul.

In all there are forty-three species of fish in the river. Some are estuarine, some are imported and some are very small. Only twenty-three of the species complete their full cycle of life in the river and, again, not all of these are native.

Dams, weirs, irrigation channels, salinity, pollution and the carp have taken a huge toll in the river-fish population. However, we are still able to get, from time to time, some decent Murray cods and Murray perch. Red fin is not a native, but I love it. Occasionally I have had catfish delivered from private waterways.

And what about the carp? Eat it, that's what I say. Eat it after carefully removing the bones. It's good. If you can eat shark, you can eat carp.

Murray Perch con Origano
Murray Perch with Oregano

Known as callop in South Australia, this is a fish that suits various Asian preparations where freshwater fish is required. I have taken this recipe from the Italian community of Mildura. It employs strong, dried oregano, grated cheese and the squeezed pulp of the ripest tomatoes.

Serves 4

PREPARATION TIME: 15 MINUTES
COOKING TIME: 5 MINUTES

1 tablespoon olive oil

4 perch fillets

salt and pepper

a big pinch of dried oregano (Greek quality)

4 teaspoons grated cheese (for example, pecorino)

4 teaspoons crushed tomato pulp

Preheat the oven to 180°C (350°F).

Rub a baking dish with oil. Place the fillets on the oil, sprinkle with dried oregano, salt and pepper, cheese and tomato pulp. Bake for less than 5 minutes in the oven and it will be ready. Perch cooks quickly.

Insalata Tiepida di Red Fin
Warm Salad of Red Fin

I love the look of red fin. It is not a native of the Murray, but we may as well treat it as one. It is also becoming rare.

Serves 2–3

PREPARATION TIME:
COOKING TIME: 15 MINUTES
FOR A LARGE FISH

1 large (600 g/20 oz) red fin

mixed green salad leaves

light olive oil

salt

verjuice

Red fin has a tough skin. If you cook it with the skin on, this forms a natural heat chamber in which the flesh will cook neatly. So cook the fish on a tray in the oven at 180° C (350° F) for 10–15 minutes.

Then remove the skin at once and take the flesh from the bone. Do it quickly, put the meat over tender green leaves and dress at once with a dressing made with a light olive oil, salt and verjuice (the juice of green grapes available from most delis), known as *agresto* in Italian.

Sunday Fishing on the Sile

Dad and his friends used to go fishing on the Sile River on a Sunday morning after church. I would watch them from the river bank. The Sile is a fast-running course which flows into the Venetian Lagoon a few kilometres downstream.

Most of the guys in the small dinghy didn't know how to swim. What would have happened if the boat capsized? Some of the old boys must have been over 100 kilograms. I reckon they would have sunk like lead.

As it was, the boat miraculously stayed afloat on each occasion.

These expeditions were accompanied by a bottle of *grappa* and much hilarity. The fishing was good too. Mostly pike, tench and some carp. My dad hung his share of the catch on the bike's handlebar and made his way home with dangling fish. This was scaled, washed and dunked in hot fat, and was served with fried potatoes. That's how I got a taste for carp.

THE MIRACLE OF THE MURRAY COD

'I'll come to the Mildura Arts Festival', read a card from Les Murray, 'if you give me a feed of Murray cod.'

I replied: 'By hook or by crook, I shall get you one — do come.'

Now here is a great Australian who knows the value of food. No money talk, food talk first. That's real sprawl, as he would say. No low dive here into the subject of agent fees, travel costs and the like. 'Just give me a feed of cod and we'll worry about the rest later.' What style!

It was a lean year, 1995, and the Chinese were paying top dollars for whole cod. However, after a bit of screaming and carrying on I got a couple of serves from the local fishmonger and placed them in the freezer. I had no choice in the matter because you cannot organise a cod *a piacere*, at your leisure.

When the writers arrived for the festival they decided to have dinner together and Les joined them with his wife, Valery, and two of his boys. How was I to feed cod only to him? You have to visualise the table with Les at one end and many other distinguished identities around him. How uncouth to provide for one and not for the rest? What if they, too, wanted their cod? So I temporised, like a politician holding a broken promise at bay for a little longer.

More fettuccine, Les? Signora Valery, more risotto? And the young ones? Have they had enough to drink? And so it went on Thursday and Friday, for breakfast, lunch and dinner. By Saturday I was a wreck. In the kitchen at 11 a.m. I slowly gained consciousness after a busy night. In the cold light of day with a badly managed promise hovering over my head like a Damocles sword, the panic mounted. Outside, the party was getting ready for lunch under the Bisleri Acqua Minerale umbrellas. George, the breakfast chef, casually said: 'Oh, I nearly forgot to tell you. The fisherman came in this morning. I didn't have time to weigh the fish. He did it all himself and got the money from reception.' The rest of his words were cut off by the slamming of the coolroom door behind me. In a state of frenzy I surveyed all the shelves and there it was, shining in its freshness, resting on one side, 8.5 kilograms, flanked by some perch for good measure, a whole cod. A gift of chance, cornucopia of the brown god of T. S. Eliot.

I prepared the fish in *bella vista* and took it outside to the assembled party. After I explained the reasons for my anxiety, we proclaimed the miracle of the fish, took pictures and ate the lot that very evening.

Murray Cod alla Grand Hotel
MURRAY COD IN THE STYLE OF THE GRAND HOTEL

Serves 4

COOKING TIME: 10 MINUTES

4 x 150 g (5 oz) cod fillets

plain (all-purpose) flour for dusting

salt and pepper

olive oil

butter

a pinch of finely chopped garlic

½ cup peeled and diced tomato

Preheat the oven to 180° C (350° F).

Lightly flour the fish slices. It is always a good idea to put a little salt and pepper in the flour and have it well mixed.

When the oil and butter are hot in the pan add the fish, cook it lightly on one side and turn over. Add the garlic and tomatoes. Keep cooking for 1 more minute and place the pan in the oven. If the heat is gentle and the pan hot, the fish will cook and the butter will not separate. If the butter splits and it looks oily, take the fish out, tip out some of the oily butter, add a few small butter cubes and stir them in. Cook for a few minutes or until ready.

Serve at once with spinach or mashed potato.

Murray Cod coi Carciofi
MURRAY COD WITH ARTICHOKES

I once cooked this dish for my friend the food writer Maggie Beer, and she loved it so much that she put it in her book. I was so flattered! You can successfully substitute blue eye cod or Spanish mackerel.

Serves 4

COOKING TIME: 6 MINUTES

MORE TO PREPARE THE ARTICHOKES

4 cooked whole artichokes with their juice (see page 112)

4 x 200 g (6 oz) pieces cod

butter

salt and pepper

a little extra-virgin olive oil

Preheat the oven to 180° C (350° F).

Place the cooked artichokes in the centre of a baking pan together with a cup of their cooking juice.

Place the medallions of fish all around and scatter a few dollops of butter over them. Add salt and pepper and drizzle in a small amount of extra-virgin olive oil. Bake in the oven until ready — it should not take more than 6 minutes.

FILLET OF CARP

The maligned carp is not bad eating at all. Get some from a specialist fish shop and fillet it.
Carefully pluck the bones with tweezers and then slice the flesh in escalopes.

Serves 4
PREPARATION TIME: 30 MINUTES
COOKING TIME: 5 MINUTES
4 tablespoons olive oil
2 tablespoons butter
12 escalopes of carp, lightly floured
3 tablespoons verjuice

Heat the olive oil and butter and add the carp to the pan. Cook the fish on both sides and add the verjuice. Cook until the fish is ready, about 5 minutes since it is a soft fish.

KOORONG MULLET

This fish comes from the salty end of the Murray. Technically it is not a river fish, but the end of the river's journey. Its flesh is darkish, a little oily and flavoursome. Fillets I have bought in Adelaide fish shops were perfectly trimmed, leaving very few bones.

I fry them gently without flour and serve them on a bed of blanched, small broad (fava) beans tossed with oil, garlic and diced tomato. Tear some fresh parsley and scatter on top.

CATFISH

This fish has an extraordinary texture. It is called by some the 'crayfish of the poor', the same expression I have heard for monkfish. In the past I have had diners who have sent it back because they didn't like its texture which proves that you cannot please them all.

Pan-fry in olive oil and finish with a dash of verjuice and extra butter.

It is not easy these days to get catfish and now it may even be a protected species in some rivers.

Fillet of Carp with Vegetables

Totani e Piselli in Umido

STEWED SQUID WITH PEAS

There are calamari and cuttlefish and then there are squids. These are brownish and cheap.
They are ideal for stewing with tomatoes and peas.

Serves 6

PREPARATION TIME: 1 HOUR
COOKING TIME: 1 HOUR

1 kg (2 lb) squid
1 large onion, chopped
5 cloves garlic, chopped
olive oil
60 mL (¼ cup) white wine
500 g (1 lb) crushed, peeled tomatoes
400 g (14 oz) peas (canned will do)
chopped Italian (flat-leaf) parsley
chilli flakes

To clean the squid, pull out the tentacles and remove the beak and guts. Cut off the suckers that may be too tough and remove the wings at the bottom of the tube. Rinse, then cut into small pieces.

Fry the onion and garlic in olive oil, add the squid and simmer. Add the wine, let it evaporate and add the tomatoes and peas. Cook on a low heat for about 1 hour or until tender and the taste is concentrated.

Add parsley and chilli flakes if desired.

Razza e Polenta
Skate Stew with Polenta

I was thrilled to eat some skate in the Chinese quarter in Kuala Lumpur from a street vendor at two in the morning! I wanted to throw myself into the street food experience in KL immediately upon arrival, which was at midnight.

From the hotel to the street vendors we had to run the gauntlet of an interminable line of amazing-looking boys who wanted to be girls. I had to explain that I had other fish to fry. They giggled and did not believe that I was out at that hour for serious food reasons.

The skate was cooked on a banana leaf placed on a hotplate which is inclined backward so that the cook can quickly and deftly scoop up the very hot oil that gathers against the side of the hotplate and pour it constantly over the skate. This method of cooking and the spices used made it a memorable dish. In this recipe the skate is simply cooked with tomato.

Serves 6

PREPARATION TIME: 1 HOUR
COOKING TIME: 40 MINUTES

1 onion, chopped

olive oil

3 cloves garlic, chopped

1 tablespoon minced chilli

1 kg (2 lb) stingray, cleaned of fibrous parts and skin, cut into large chunks

60 mL (¼ cup) white wine

1 x 400 g (14 oz) can tomatoes

extra olive oil

½ cup Italian (flat-leaf parsley)

olives, to taste

capers, to taste

Fry the onion in olive oil until translucent and add the garlic and chilli. Add the fish and the white wine.

In the meantime in a separate pan make a quick tomato sauce with the tomatoes, a little oil and nothing else. Combine the sauce and the skate and cook for about 30 minutes or until ready. Add the parsley, and then the olives and capers in small quantities during the last phase of cooking.

Serve with polenta or fresh spinach.

If you omit the olives and capers, you can accompany this dish with the Asian swamp cabbage, *kangkong*, quickly stir-fried with *belachan* (shrimp paste).

You can also add any leftover tomato sauce over a bowl of spaghetti.

DOLCI E BISCOTTI
SWEETS AND BISCUITS

It is always difficult to present a dessert section in an Italian cookery book. In many books I have read, recipes in this section swing violently from the esoteric to the banal. In some ways this reflects the regional character — hence the fragmentation — of Italian food and the secondary importance of dessert in societies where subsistence agriculture was the main activity.

Where the Italians excel in dessert-making is in the patisserie. You go there and buy ready-made desserts and ice-creams. Another area of excellence — although one that industrial society has almost destroyed — comprises a myriad of biscuits and other *pasticcini* such as fritters and deep-fried pastries and 'weird' things like robinia flowers and sweetened pig's blood.

Fruit is used extensively for cooked desserts or eaten fresh. In eight years of cooking, day in and day out, I have had one request for fresh fruit after dinner, and it came from some visiting Italian businessmen. A bowl of perfect cherries or glistening grapes or sweet navel oranges in the winter — not to mention the tropical fruit available in Australia — can make a grand finale to a dinner. Yet, no one would regard it as such. We demand our puddings and do not teach our kids to eat fruit. If we were to eat a few more oranges, citrus trees would not need to be pulled out. It is as simple as that.

The quest for good desserts has prompted Australian chefs to borrow from the British, French, Italian, American, and now even the Asian tradition. They are now creating some spectacular desserts. I too have allowed some poetic licence in the sweets and desserts you will find in this section.

FOR WHOM THE BELL TOLLS

I came to Australia from a small paese called Casier which comprises, in its municipal boundaries, another village called Dosson. My family always had a foot in each place, but my personal memories – and attractions – tend to return to Casier where I went to school, church and where I finally returned to get married. Casier, like Mildura, is located on the banks of a river, the Sile, a fast running course which flows into the Venetian Lagoon a few kilometres downstream. The Sile is a kind of waterway into the former Serene Republic of Venice, also known as La Serenissima, The Most Serene.

Casier is located a few kilometres from the town of Altino, which faces the marshes of the lagoon. It is from there, as the story goes, that the refugees escaped the hordes of Attila, took to hiding in the lagoon and finally adopted it as their permanent place of residence, establishing a Republic that lasted more than one thousand years.

The influence of Venice is obvious throughout the countryside – in the monuments, the villas, the parks, the churches and other public buildings – and in the cooking, although each regional centre developed its own style.

In Casier the influence of Venice was direct: from her port came the barges laden with various types of seeds that went to an oil factory on the other side of the river. These barges were very colourful: vivid blue, yellow, red, green and black and entire families lived in them.

The influence of the barcari, the boat people, made Casier a Communist village, despite being in the heart of the most Catholic, Christian Democratic part of Italy.

You could tell who was Communist. If they listened with deliberate intent to Radio Istria, located in former Communist Yugoslavia, which used to broadcast in Italian, they had to be Reds. Radio Istria used to have a listeners' request program for people celebrating a birthday or an anniversary. A radio announcer would say something like this: 'The children of Giuseppe Vatteloapesca — Mario, Delfina, Umberto, united with their cousins so and so, and the neighbours so and so, from the town of so and so, request the song "The Red Flag" to honour their father, Giuseppe, on the felicitous occasion of his birthday.' And thereupon 'The Red Flag' would scream out of the radio for all to listen. As all farmers had lunch at the same time, and all listened to Radio Istria in unison because some of the songs requested were pop hits of the day, 'The Red Flag' could be heard resonating from farm to farm for thousands of square kilometres — in fact, right through the north-east, much to the chagrin of my father, who was a card-carrying Christian Democrat member and local town councillor.

'Turn down the volume of that radio!' he used to bark.

Casier held its annual (Communist) Festival dell'Unita, which consisted, rather modestly, of a large dancing floor laid out in the middle of a paddock with a tarp over it in case of rain. An orchestra would play, food was prepared and a politically incorrect Miss Festival dell'Unita was chosen late in the evening. A fairly drab affair. Needless to say that for the community of benpensanti, the right-thinking people, this girl had loose morals. And the priest, Don Ruben, who was still there to celebrate my wedding in 1991, would thunder from the pulpit that he would excommunicate all those taking part in La Festa, especially the girl elected Miss Festa dell'Unita.

This Don Camillo stuff is rather funny in retrospect, but it was serious then, at least in my eyes. Funnier still is an accident that had me turn dear Don Ruben into a veritable rebel. When I went to Casier to get married, I discovered that I had to get permission from the Curia, the local Bishop Office. There I was interrogated by an arrogant pipsqueak who asked for a document of approval from the Curia in Melbourne. No document, no consent to a church wedding. I showed him the nulla osta from both parishes, mine and that of my wife-to-be, thinking that would suffice. That didn't satisfy this Inquisition zealot.

I turned to Don Ruben with anxiety: 'We have relations from Australia and from various parts of Italy coming here on Sunday. What are we going to do?'

To which, the old priest said, 'Stuff the Bishop's Office. I have known you since you were a child and I will ring the bells to announce your wedding.' *Suonero le campane*, he said. For me it was a very special day when my old priest rebelled against the bureaucrats. As it turned out, we were able to obtain the documentation — not without some effort — and have it certified. I wouldn't have put the old boy's resolve to the test anyway, lest he might excommunicate himself!

Panna Cotta al Caramello
Caramelised Panna Cotta

This idea was given to me by my friend Francesco Benvenuti, a wonderful chef who lives in a remote part of Mexico and occasionally comes to visit us in Mildura. It was used for a dinner prepared by Francesco and Maggie Beer at the Mildura Literature Prize in 1998 to accompany poached quinces. The Philip Hodgins Memorial Medal that year went to Bruce Dawe, who had the public in fits of laughter with his poems on football and footballers.

Panna cotta is best made the day before and chilled. It is good by itself or with stewed or poached fruit. This dessert is one that Maggie Beer and Stephanie Alexander have named the ultimate panna cotta. Maggie says that you have to do it a few times to develop a relationship with it. I think she is right, but then tell me of a good dessert that does not require that commitment!

Serves 12

PREPARATION TIME: 30 MINUTES
COOKING TIME: 1 HOUR 45 MINUTES

1 L (4 cups) cream
1 vanilla bean
zest of ½ lemon
zest of ½ orange
1 small piece cinnamon
4 coffee beans
½ cup castor (superfine) sugar
10 egg whites

CARAMEL
2 cups sugar
100 mL (scant ½ cup) water

Scald the cream with the vanilla, the zests, cinnamon, coffee beans and sugar. Allow the sugar to dissolve, then cool and strain.

To make the caramel, place sugar in a small pot with the water. This water should melt all the sugar. Boil until golden or very similar to honey in colour.

Pour 8 mm (⅓ inch) of this caramel into separate dariole moulds.

Preheat the oven to 170°C (320°F).

Beat the egg whites to stiff peaks and fold swiftly into the cooled cream, making sure everything is evenly mixed. Pour the mixture into the moulds but not right up to the top. Leave room for the mixture to rise (and it will fall).

Place the moulds in a water bath in the oven for 5 minutes and then reduce the heat to 140°C (280°F) and bake for 1 ½ hours or until firm.

PANNA COTTA AL GORGONZOLA
PANNA COTTA WITH BLUE CHEESE

If you remove the blue cheese you have a straight panna cotta *that suits all kinds of fruits and berries. It can be found in many a restaurant but I have experienced far too many that taste 'hoofy', that is, of too much dried gelatine. It seems that chefs lose their nerve and fear that their* panna cotta *will not set. As gelatine is made from bones too much may cause an unpleasant smell and taste. I prefer a German-made gelatine that comes in 2-gram sheets rather than the granular product found in supermarkets.*

The addition of blue cheese came as an inspiration one day to my second chef, Aaron Evans, who could not stop fiddling with things in my absence.

'Chief,' he said, 'if they eat cheese with quince paste let's put the cheese in the panna cotta *and serve it with poached quinces.' And why not? When I tasted it I thought we had a winner.*

Serves 12

PREPARATION TIME: 20 MINUTES
SETTING TIME: 8 HOURS

1 L (4 cups) cream

1 vanilla bean

4 coffee beans

1 small cinnamon stick

1 small piece lemon zest

1 small piece orange zest

2 tablespoons blue cheese, such as a good gorgonzola

¼ cup palm sugar

2 sheets gelatine

Place the cream and vanilla bean, coffee beans, cinnamon stick and zests in a pan on the heat and scald — do not let it boil. Crumble the cheese and palm sugar into the scalded cream. Keep tasting because cheese varies a lot. This cream should have just a delicate hint of cheese and should not be too sweet. (With this recipe I am giving you very conservative quantities.)

Soften and dissolve the gelatine in warm water and stir into the cream. Strain into a bowl through a fine sieve. Taste again — you can still add this or that while the cream is warm. Cool in the bowl, stirring from time to time. Place the whole in the refrigerator or pour into individual moulds and chill.

CASSATA
ITALIAN-STYLE ICE-CREAM

*This summer dessert is in the semi-freddo family. You can change the content and follow the same procedure —
the possibilities are endless. You can complicate the recipe by including the traditional hazelnut praline. Add it,
if you wish, even though the result may be a little too sweet (³/₄ cup hazelnuts to ¹/₂ sugar). I have also given a
recipe for a large quantity. It is not worth doing this in a small amount because it is a frozen dessert —
hence you can store it in moulds or logs and always have an impressive dessert at your service.*

I do not like this dessert with any other embellishments, but I admit that it looks a little stark on a plate by itself.

Serves 18
PREPARATION TIME: 1 HOUR

¹/₃ cup sultanas, soaked in 2 tablespoons
brown rum

200 g (7 oz) egg whites (from about 6 eggs)

1 cup sugar

¹/₂ cup candied fruits (citron, angelica,
cherries, etc.)

¹/₃ cup pistachios, unsalted, crushed coarsely

1.5 L (6 cups) semi-whipped cream

Macerate sultanas for at least two hours.

Whip egg whites to soft peaks and while that is happening bring the sugar to a temperature of 120°C (250°F). You do not need a sugar thermometer, but if you have one be scientific by all means. At 120°C the sugar has melted, is still white and is bubbling happily.

Add the hot sugar to the egg whites with the beater going at high speed. The sugar will cook the egg whites. Slow the machine to medium and keep slowing until the mixture has cooled.

Fold the candied fruits and pistachios into the cream, gently, and equally gently fold in the egg whites, making sure that all is well amalgamated.

Pour into moulds (plastic ones are cheap, or into tins). Freeze for at least 8 hours. It is best to wait a few minutes before serving to allow it to soften.

Torta al Cioccolato e Olio di Oliva

OLIVE OIL CHOCOLATE CAKE

This is an amazing cake for cheats. The oil keeps it very moist, but instead of real chocolate you use drinking chocolate powder.

Serves 10

PREPARATION TIME: 15 MINUTES
COOKING TIME: 20–30 MINUTES

7 eggs, separated

1 cup castor (superfine) sugar

425 mL (1 2/3 cups) extra-virgin olive oil

1 cup self-raising flour, sifted

1 3/4 cups drinking chocolate
(not cocoa), sifted

125 mL (1/2 cup) warm water

1/4 cup sugar when beating egg whites

Preheat the oven to 180°C (350°F).

Beat egg yolks with castor sugar until fluffy. If the mixture tends to be thick, add 1 tablespoon of warm water. This will help the mixture turn fluffy again.

With the beater on medium speed add olive oil, bit by bit, like making mayonnaise. Add dry ingredients to the mixture on low speed and beat until all combined. Add the water.

Whip the egg whites until thick, add the sugar and beat until it dissolves.

Pour chocolate mixture into a large bowl and gently but swiftly fold in the egg whites. When well combined pour into a greased 23 cm (9 inch) cake tin and bake for 1 hour or until cooked.

Torta di Polenta con Semi di Finocchio
POLENTA CAKE WITH FENNEL SEEDS

This is a rich cake that is best eaten cold the day after. In Venetian dialect it is called pinza or pinsa, a cake associated with the festivities around the day of the Epiphany, 6 January. This is the day when the Three Kings pay a visit to little Jesus bearing gifts of gold, frankincense and myrrh.

On the eve of the Epiphany, the night of 5 January, it was traditional to light a big bonfire to illuminate the path for the Three Kings. Organising the bonfire could take up to ten days. Mind you, farmers had little to do during that time of the year and so they indulged their kids with this little extravaganza. First, we'd fell a very tall tree and truncate by half the main branches. This trunk was then driven into a hole in the ground as a kind of giant coat hanger. When it was secure, we'd start placing burning material on the top branches — usually bundles of dry grass or sticks, bicycle tyres, old boots, car tyres, anything inflammable — and work our way down. Only when the pile was huge were we satisfied. Sometimes this was a collective effort — by a village competing for the tallest bonfire — sometimes it was the effort of a few children or a father and child.

Either way, when the fires were lit that evening the countryside looked magical, especially when it was covered with snow. You'd hear kids screaming with laughter, adults calling each other and singing silly rhymes like: 'Pan e vin, pan e vin, a pinsa xe soto el camin' ('Bread and wine, bread and wine, the pinsa (cake) is on the fire'). If the sparks went straight up that was an omen for a good year to come. Back at the house after the bonfire, we'd eat pinsa with coffee, grappa or wine.

This pinsa was not home-made. It was prepared by the baker who could produce it on baking tins of 1 m by 2 m (3 feet by 6 feet). My father, like all the other blokes, had a two-wheeled cart that he could attach to the back of his bike, under the seat. That is what he used to transport the pinsa from the baker's shop to our house. And so did everyone else. So it was that before the Epiphany there were many men with two-wheeled carts loaded with pinsa pedalling around the countryside.

The recipe given here is a lot better than the cake of my childhood, which seemed to taste only of bread and aniseeds.

Serves 6 people or more

PREPARATION TIME: 1 HOUR
COOKING TIME: 30 MINUTES

1/3 cup sultanas

1 cup chopped dried figs and other glacé fruit
such as peaches and apricots

1/3 cup pinenuts

1 teaspoon fennel seeds

2 nips (60 mL) grappa

2 cups yellow polenta (cornmeal)

1 1/2 cups plain (all-purpose) flour

milk

2/3 cup sugar

6 tablespoons butter

Infuse sultanas, dried fruits, pinenuts and fennel seeds with *grappa*.

Combine the two flours in a heavy casserole and add as much milk as you need to obtain a smooth and soft mixture, like making polenta. Place the mixture on a moderate heat and cook for 15 minutes, stirring all the time.

Preheat the oven to 180°C (350°F).

Add sugar and butter and the marinating ingredients. Mix well and pour into a heavy baking dish with fairly high sides or a large, buttered and floured cake tin.

Bake in the oven for about 35 minutes. Turn out onto a cake grille to let cool. I like serving a small portion of *pinsa* with whipped cream.

Torta della Nonna

ALMOND AND CUSTARD CAKE

*This dessert is a classic, but somehow it now seems forgotten. Italian custard is made with a small amount
of flour as the thickening agent and once you have learnt to make it you can go on and prepare* zuppa inglese,
which is not a soup at all but a trifle (see page 203).

*Torta della nonna is essentially a pie: a flan base is lined with sweet dough, filled with custard and closed
with a lid of the same pastry over which you scatter slivered almonds and pinenuts.*

There are many recipes for thick custard, known by the French as crème pattisiere. *Strangely enough they
all seem to work! I tend to go for a middle-of-the-road version that does not rely on either too many eggs, too much
sugar or flour. There is also a school of cooking that replaces plain (all-purpose) flour with cornflour (cornstarch).
Fool around a bit, change proportions and see what happens.*

Serves 10
PREPARATION TIME: 30 MINUTES
COOKING TIME: 10–15 MINUTES

PASTRY
200 g (7 oz) butter
²/₃ cup castor (superfine) sugar
2 eggs
3 cups plain (all-purpose) flour
¹/₂ cup almonds and pinenuts

CUSTARD
1 L (4 cups) milk
1 vanilla bean, or some essence
a few pieces orange and lemon zest
3 egg yolks
2 eggs
¹/₂ cup castor (superfine) sugar
¹/₂ cup plain (all-purpose) flour

For the pastry, lightly cream the butter and sugar and add the eggs. Add the flour, knead gently and refrigerate until cold.

For the custard, bring the milk to the boil with the vanilla bean and zests. Beat the egg yolks and eggs lightly with the sugar and flour. Add a little of the hot milk and blend it in. Strain the rest of the milk into the egg mixture, return to the heat in an appropriate pot and cook until thickened. Make sure it does not stick to the bottom, as it can easily do just to infuriate you. When thickened I usually give it about 2 minutes of bubbling and then I pour it onto a cold bench, spread it out with a spatula and work it and rework it until it cools. That way it will not form a 'skin', which is not a big drama anyway.

Preheat the oven to 180°C (350°F).

Roll out the pastry and line a 20cm (8 inch) tart ring leaving a little extra dough hanging over so that you can fold it back inside after you have filled the tart with custard. Fill the tart with custard. With a brush apply a little water to the pastry edge and fold back over the custard.

Roll out another disc of pastry and press it around the border.

Sprinkle with nuts and bake for 35–40 minutes or until golden. When cold decorate with icing sugar and serve with whipped cream or even vanilla ice-cream.

A SUNDAY EVENING OUT IN
NORTH MELBOURNE, CIRCA 1974

It was a beautiful, still, Sunday evening, at the end of March 1974. I had been in Australia three days and my hosts had left me alone in their house to acclimatise. I had slept, mostly, as jet-lag affects me badly. But in the back of my mind, as a young Italian boy, well dressed, a svelte 64 kilograms, was the notion of going out, like in Italy, on this Sunday evening. And I could see the lights of the city from the balcony at 22 Shiel Street, North Melbourne, beckoning me or my young genital apparatus or whatever it is that makes young people want to 'go out'.

So I put on my Sunday best, just like in Italy the week before, including, I remember, a very light raincoat because it was, as we say in Italy, *mezza stagione*, the middle of the season, and I was conscious that any variation in temperature not dealt with appropriately shows one to possess a limited wardrobe at best or, at worst, pure bad taste!

Looking like a dandy, I exited 22 Shiel Street, turned confidently to the left towards the city, and began my walk. Soon I realised that no-one, and I mean no-one, was promenading. an empty tram rattled past, a car slowed for the lights, a figure popped out of some poorly illuminated flats to be gobbled up again by the darkness. A sense of solitude overwhelmed me until I saw a corner building with a rotating blue sign on its roof and another blue sign above its door. I knew that that was the symbol for a pub: the legendary, friendly pub, where people meet, have a beer and chat, as described in the English-language textbook at secondary school, in reference to England. Never mind, England, Australia, it was all the same to me that day. I pushed the doors of this establishment but they didn't open. I very nearly hurt my head when the doors didn't give way.

I persuaded myself that this place must have been closed on Sunday as each pub must take a day off — the infamous *chiusura di turno* that tourists hate so much about Italy. I was being administered a dose of the same medicine. I did not know pubs were closed on Sunday in Victoria. So I pushed on, and on and on. Each pub, same story. And there were lots of pubs in North Melbourne in 1974. I even went around to the back of one and soon abandoned that enterprise when two ferocious dogs leapt against a metal fence, jolting me out of my wits.

Eventually, on a main road with a tram line and a full view of what later I understood to be the North Melbourne Town Hall, I saw an illuminated sign, and a person coming out of that particular establishment. I was in luck, I thought. As I quickly reached my goal, I read what the sign announced. It said: MILK BAR.

I said to myself, 'Bugger the milk, let's go for the bar.' So I pushed open a dirty door with mesh wire and suddenly set off an alarm! I entered cautiously, casting my eyes from left to right, and in front of me. I saw some limp celery, a bag of spuds, some lonely tomatoes on a shelf. Still, I thought, a bar is a bar. In Italy a bar is a bar. Sure, in some remote villages it functions as a bazaar, like here perhaps. A fat man with a five o'clock shadow that went on to midnight came out of the back and approached the same bench I was aiming for. Even before I got there I said, 'A beer, please.'

The fellow looked at me, looked at me again, his face not showing any emotions, until he said, in Italian, 'How long have you been in Australia?'

'A few days', I replied. He said, 'Follow me.' At the back of the shop was a kind of lounge room where his very fat son was watching a black-and-white television sprawled on a vinyl couch with the plastic packaging still on it. The fellow pulled open the fridge door and took out a bottle of Melbourne Bitter, a favourite with the Italians from North Melbourne to Thomastown, because they had acquired a taste for its sweetness, and they could recycle the bottles for home-made tomato sauce. (With the recent advent of screw-top bottles, apparently you cannot apply the metal cap so necessary for Italian home-made preserves.) We had a beer together, I was introduced to his wife, they asked me a few pertinent questions and after a second glass, I was dispatched home.

I didn't visit a pub for at least a year after that memorable experience.

Next time I did go into a pub was when I went to buy a bottle of wine at Young and Jackson on the corner of Flinders and Swanston streets. I was young and immature and while I knew by and large what a wine should taste like I was not as fanatical (or financial) about it as I am now. In Italy we made our own, and pretty well, too, so we drank wine all the time and did not give any thought to it.

At the bottle shop I asked for the best bottle of wine they had and a lad gave me a bottle of Queen Adelaide claret. Now, you have to admit that at a time when most people drank beer and Ben Ean Moselle, to graduate to Queen Adelaide was something. You can all act like smart foodies and experienced wine buffs out there, but I am old enough to remember what the nation used to drink; Queen Ad was a bit ordinary, but not bad in that context. Besides, I was going out to dinner without knowing if the hosts drank wine at all — why risk taking a bottle that could disappear into the cupboard until next Christmas?

So it was that I turned up for dinner at a nice establishment in Armadale and consigned the bottle in the brown paper bag to the hostess soon after the preliminary greetings. She took a glance at the bottle and the bloody thing disappeared straight into a cupboard.

'Oh, shit,' I thought. 'Another place where I cannot have a glass of wine. I bet these buggers don't even put bread on the table.' No wine and no bread are the ingredients for an Italian nightmare. Add to it a tuna casserole and a serious nervous breakdown is in order.

I was offered a pre-dinner drink of some kind and soon after, the party of five moved into the dining room. There, on a sideboard, were perfect wine glasses, decanters and at least five bottles with the corks resting next to them. I kept my cool and moved near to read the labels nonchalantly: Château Latour. Château Margaux. Grange.

Torta d'Arancio
Sunraysia Orange Cake

A fairly heavy citrus-based dessert. I suggest that you serve it after a light dinner.

Serves 10

PREPARATION TIME: 1 1/2 HOURS
COOKING TIME: 55 MINUTES

2 small oranges

125 g (4 oz) butter

1 cup castor (superfine) sugar

3 eggs, separated

1/2 teaspoons cinnamon

1 1/2 cups almond meal

1/2 cup self-raising flour

1/2 teaspoons baking powder

Cook the oranges (whole) in water for 1 hour or until soft. (This can be done ahead of time or in the microwave to save time.) Remove from the water and cut in half. Remove any pips. Blend the oranges to a paste.

Preheat the oven to 180°C (350°F).

Cream butter and sugar until fluffy. Add the egg yolks and mix well. Mix cinnamon, almond meal, flour and baking powder into the mixture on low speed. Fold orange paste into the mixture.

Beat the egg whites until stiff and fold them into the mixture.

Pour the mixture into a 23 cm (9 inch) tin greased with butter and dusted with flour and bake for 45–55 minutes.

This cake will never really dry up because the orange paste is 'wet'. It will always be a little sticky like a pudding. You an even serve it hot with double cream or ice-cream.

ARANCE SANGUIGNE AL CARAMELLO
CARAMELISED BLOOD ORANGES

This dessert stands on its own, but it can be served with cream or with a normal panna cotta *(see page 188).*
It is best in the winter when blood oranges are available — you can also use navels. It can be made ahead.

Serves 6

PREPARATION TIME: 30 MINUTES
COOKING TIME: 15 MINUTES

8–10 blood or navel oranges
(make sure they are sweet)

1 dried bay leaf, crumbled

a few cloves

1 stick cinnamon

3 cups sugar

250 mL (1 cup) water

250 mL (1 cup) freshly squeezed orange juice

Peel the oranges, and remove all pith. Slice into 5 mm (¼ inch) discs and remove any core. Place overlapping slices in a container — preferably stainless steel, but not plastic — and scatter over the roughly crumbled bay leaf, cloves and cinnamon stick.

Place sugar and water in a pan, making sure that all the sugar is wet. Put on a high heat, and remember to keep the sides of the pan free of sugar to avoid the formation of crystals, which will ruin the process. To do this brush the insides of the pan with water using a clean pastry brush.

When the sugar has turned into a lovely golden-honey colour add the fresh orange juice and bring back to the boil. Remember that it is going to spit so be ready with a lid and be careful not to burn yourself.

Strain the caramel and pour it over the oranges. The taste improves if you let it sit overnight. It keeps for at least 2 days in the refrigerator.

ZUPPA INGLESE
ITALIAN TRIFLE

Zuppa inglese, literally English Soup, is really a trifle, and there is nothing to it. While it has been done to death in every book of Italian cuisine, it is not as if you go out to dinner and scores of people are chasing you with a serve of zuppa inglese, is it? So I'd like to re-propose this simple dessert — it is fun and reminds you how to make a delicious sponge.

Serves 10
PREPARATION TIME: 1 1/2 HOURS
COOKING TIME:

SPONGE
6 eggs
1 ¼ cups castor (superfine) sugar
1 cup plain (all-purpose) flour, sifted
½ cup cornflour (cornstarch), sifted
1 ½ teaspoons baking powder, sifted
2 tablespoons melted butter

FILLING
rum
1 cup sugar syrup (made by dissolving
½ sugar cup in ½ cup water over a low heat)
1 quantity Custard (see page 196)
Alchermes
3 egg whites
¼ cup castor (superfine) sugar
candied fruit, finely diced

Preheat the oven to 180°C (350°F).

For the sponge, beat the eggs until thick and creamy — they will more than double in volume. Gradually add the sugar and beat in until it has dissolved.

Gently fold in the other sponge ingredients without making lumps or losing the air in the eggs.

Pour into a 20 x 30 cm (8 x 12 inch) baking tray or a 27 cm (10 inch) round cake tin, depending on the shape you want to work with. I find it easier to line the cake tin with foil. Bake for about 20–25 minutes in a moderate oven.

When the sponge is ready and cooled, cut horizontally into three layers. Place the first layer in a suitable dish — square or round as long as it has sides. Pour some rum diluted with a little sugar syrup over the sponge.

Cover the sponge with custard. Place another layer of sponge on top which you can wet with an Italian liqueur called Alchermes (available from bottleshops run by Italians) diluted with sugar syrup, and continue until you finish the sponge. Make sure each layer of sponge is made moist by the rum or Alchermes, and sugar syrup.

Whip three fresh egg whites to a firm meringue with the sugar. Spread over the cake and sprinkle with finely diced candied fruit. Place briefly in a 190°C (375°F) heat oven to dry the meringue a little or even to colour it. You can do without the meringue and replace it with whipped cream.

Bocconotti di Ricotta
Ricotta Parcel

There are many variations on ricotta as this cheese was readily available to all in the past and continues to be available commercially all over the world. This recipe requires a baking tray with sides no higher than 2 cm (³/4 in). You can line the baking tray with foil to make it easier to remove the cake. The attractive feature of this cake is that you can flavour the ricotta pretty much as you like: with candied fruits, but also with chocolate or citrus-based concoctions or toasted almonds.

Serves 10
PREPARATION TIME: 1 HOURS
COOKING TIME: 30 MINUTES

PASTRY
2 cups plain (all-purpose) flour
140 g (4 ¹/2 oz) butter
³/4 cup sugar
3 eggs
a pinch of grated lemon zest

FILLING
500 g (1 lb) fresh (but not wet) ricotta
¹/2 cup castor (superfine) sugar
¹/4 cup citron or other glacé fruit or lightly toasted and crushed almonds
3 egg yolks
1 egg

To make the pastry, mix all the ingredients and rest in the refrigerator for 30 minutes.

Preheat the oven to 180°C (350°F).

Flour the bench and rolling pin. Divide the pastry into two and roll out fairly thinly, say to 3 mm (¹/4 inch).

Lightly butter a 20 x 30 cm (8 x 10 inch) baking dish and place one piece of pastry over it keeping the pastry away from the sides.

Mix together well the ricotta and other filling ingredients, and then evenly distribute the filling over the pastry, keeping it at least 2 cm (³/4 inch) away from the side of the pastry.

Place the other piece of pastry over the filling and seal with a little egg or water. Brush a little bit of egg over the top and place in the oven. Cook for about 30 minutes or until the cake is golden brown.

Serve when cold with whipped cream. It is also a cake for breakfast or for a picnic.

Riso all'Imperatrice
The Empress Rice

An old-fashioned dessert suitable for warm days. I like the colour of candied fruits, the velvety texture
of the rice and the creaminess imparted to the dessert by the crème anglaise.

Serves 8–10

PREPARATION TIME: 1 HOUR

Rice

600 mL (2 ½ cups) milk

1 vanilla bean

¾ cup Arborio rice, boiled for
30 minutes and refreshed

a pinch of salt

2 tablespoons butter

60 g sugar

4 tablespoons apricot purée
(canned fruit will do)

½ cup candied fruit of your choice, cut into
small pieces and macerated in white rum

250 mL (1 cup) whipped cream

Crème Anglaise

800 mL (3 ¼ cups) milk

1 vanilla bean

8 egg yolks

1 cup sugar

3 sheets gelatine

To make the rice, infuse the milk with the vanilla bean
for 30 minutes. Fish out the vanilla bean.

Cook the rice in the milk with the salt, butter and
sugar for about 30 minutes or until soft. (Rice takes
longer cooking in milk and sugar.)

When the rice has cooked place it in a bowl and
blend in the apricot purée and candied fruits.

To make the *crème anglaise*, bring the milk to the boil
and infuse with the vanilla bean for 10 minutes. Beat the
yolks and sugar together, and when they are pale and
creamy add the warm milk. Put this mixture in a small
pot and cook it gently until it thickens, stirring all the
time. It may be easier and less risky to cook this custard
on a double boiler. When ready, remove about 500 mL
(2 cups) and stir in the gelatine sheets.

As the rice cools, add the *crème anglaise* in which you
have previously dissolved the gelatine. As this mixture
comes together add the whipped cream.

Spoon the whole mixture into a mould of your
choice, which has been very lightly oiled. Chill until set
and unmould onto a big plate.

Extra *crème anglaise*, whipped cream or a fruit sauce
can be served to accompany.

Frittelle di Riso e Sultana
Sultana Jelly with Sultana Rice Fritters

This is a dish that combines the rice of northern Italy with the sultana grape of Mildura.
It is a bit quirky and a lot of fun. You will see fresh sultana grapes on market stalls every year in autumn.

Serves 10
PREPARATION TIME: 1 HOUR
COOKING TIME: 30 MINUTES

Sultana Jelly
1 L (4 cups) fresh sultana juice,
strained through a fine cloth
4 scant teaspoons cornflour (cornstarch)
1 ½ teaspoons sugar

Rice Fritter dough
⅓ cup flour
40 g dry yeast
a little milk, warmed
600 mL (2 ½ cups) milk
½ cup rice
½ cup plain (all-purpose) flour, sifted
3 egg yolks
1 egg
a pinch of salt
¼ cup dried sultanas, softened with a little
grappa or water
3 teaspoons castor (superfine) sugar
grated zest of a lemon
oil for frying
icing (confectioners) sugar, for dusting

For the sultana jelly, bring the juice to the boil in a stainless-steel pot. Pour some of it into the combined cornflour and sugar and stir. Return to the pot and cook until the mixture is translucent and thick. Pour into 6 dariole moulds and chill.

For the rice fritter dough, place the flour in a bowl and put the yeast in the centre together with a little milk, about 50 mL (⅕ cup). Knead into a small ball of smooth dough, cut a cross in the dough and place it in a bowl with a couple of tablespoons of warm milk. Let it prove in a warmish place for about 20 minutes.

Bring the remaining milk to the boil, add the rice and cook it until soft but not mushy. When it is ready drain and cool it in a bowl. When just warm add the flour, the yolks and egg, salt and the dough, which by now must have doubled in size, the sultanas, fine sugar and grated lemon zest.

If the mixture appears too hard, add a little more milk. Drop spoonfuls of the mixture into hot oil, fry until golden on both sides, and drain on paper towels. Sprinkle with icing sugar.

To serve, place a jelly on a plate with one or two fritters resting on a vine leaf.

CAPPUCINO LIKE A SOUFFLÉ

Australians have taken to coffee like a duck to water. In fact, they have taken not only to coffee but to the whole notion of drinking coffee in their local *caffè* where they read the paper, or exchange gossip with friends or simply observe others doing the same. A very Italian thing, this people watching! I must confess that I am a bad offender myself but I must hasten to say that Italians look at everyone, not just women.

'Look at the fellow there with a big nose!'

'Look at that one: who does he think he is? Marcello Mastroianni forty years ago?

'And look at that one: he is always at the *caffè*, does he not do any work?'

And so on and on, forever classifying people, judging them, admiring them or belittling them.

At the *caffè* of my village, some years ago, watching people on Sunday afternoon was an extension of watching people in the church in the morning. One of my peers, for instance, used to come to church every Sunday with a completely new outfit. We'd all wait to see what he'd sport and waited to be dazzled again at the bar after lunch where he'd turn up with yet another new set of clothes.

The bar was a proper pub that also specialised in ice-cream cups: gargantuan cups, those containing at least five scoops sitting in a bath of liqueur surmounted by a generous squirt of whipped cream, various slices of fruit and a huge biscuit that looked like a Chinese fan.

You'd have to arrive fairly early after lunch to occupy a table (with your friends) in order to spend time watching others. One day, having taken up the last remaining positions with my friends, I proceeded inside the bar to get one of those ice-cream cups. Upon my return I found that my chair had been taken by one of the local bullies despite the protestations of my friends. He was significantly older and I quickly figured that if I took him on, I'd have the sympathy of the crowd, which by then was intensely focused on the loud discussion I was having with him.

'Get up and give me back my chair'.

'Go jump, stupid little kid,' he said. And thereupon I poured the contents of my ice-cream cup all over him — his head and face, his collar, his shirt and his trousers. Everyone laughed at him and he was in no position to do anything to me. Poor bugger! I am sure that he only had one set of 'Sunday best'. He must have gone home and stayed there.

The thing I find difficult to explain is The Bar because it is also a *Caffè* and sometimes this Bar and *Caffè* also has a restaurant attached to it. In my mind this 'unit' has different functions for different parts of the day. In the morning you go there for coffee — although that is legitimate also after lunch. Mid-morning you go for an aperitif or a small glass of sparkling wine. In the afternoon for a thirst quencher, whatever it may be, a digestive. In the early part of the evening for tapas and white wine. Later again for more coffee, liqueurs and even more snacks.

In Australia we now seem to have the habit of eating at any time and having cappuccino or *caffè latte* also at any time, in any season. I am not a purist by any standard, but I find this compulsive coffee-drinking as a most indecorous thing. How can you have a *caffè latte* after dinner? Have you not had enough food?

This *caffè latte* business in a glass: where did this barbarian affectation develop? *Lattè macchiato*, or spotted milk, another drink, really (a cup of espresso poured into a glass of warm milk) is traditionally served in a long glass but at a temperature that you can deal with without the fire brigade coming to your rescue. I suspect that both *caffè latte* in the glass and espresso in the glass are affectations introduced by some Romans — no offence — and the Aussies have taken to them, adding the scorching temperature. No heat, no value, the cuppa will not last as long, is that it? Or is the cuppa a heat device to keep your hands warm in the winter?

And what about cappuccino at 100 degrees with a froth that makes it look like a soufflé? Is the froth also part of the value? And who had the idea of sprinkling chocolate over the froth?

Let's get the record straight for at least those who want to go to the year 2000 and beyond with a fair idea about coffee, when you should drink it and how.

Drink espresso out of a cup, not glass. The better the cup, the better the coffee. It's the same with tea.

Don't expect cappuccino to be so hot and frothy — you are likely to kill the creaminess of the milk and to lose the fragrance of the coffee. Eliminate the intrusive chocolate powder — it is an unnecessary flavour.

Don't expect *caffè latte* in a glass. You are likely to burn yourself. It also does not taste as good as when it is served in a good-quality cup.

Have an espresso after lunch or even dinner but please do not have a *caffè latte* after a big dinner — imagine the *antipasto*, the main and the dessert rolling around in your stomach with a *caffè latte*. *Please*.

Also note that originally *caffè latte* was a breakfast food for children. The coffee was replaced by a caffeine-free surrogate derived from cereals or vegetables. I suppose it is not in anyone's interests to show how a cheap, healthy and tasty *caffè latte* can be made.

Biscotti Peperini

PEPPER BISCUITS

These biscuits set very hard when they are cooked which is why they have to be dipped into a glass of red wine or a sparkling burgundy. Red wine is better because the peperini contain a high proportion of ground black pepper, hence the name. They leave a lovely pepper taste in the mouth that is most agreeable with the taste of red wine. They are a Venetian specialty, which reflects Venice's involvement in the spice trade.

Makes 30 biscuits

PREPARATION TIME: 10 MINUTES
COOKING TIME: 10–15 MINUTES

½ cup honey

120 g (4 oz) butter

½ cup brown sugar

a pinch of nutmeg

a pinch of ground cinnamon

3 ground cloves

2 pinches of freshly ground black pepper

2 cups plain (all-purpose) flour, sifted

Over a bath of hot water dissolve the honey, butter and brown sugar, and add all the spices. Cool.

Preheat the oven to 180°C (350°F).

When mixture is cool, add the flour and work into a smooth dough. On a floured surface, roll out the dough to 3 mm (⅛ inch) thick and cut into any shape you like. Bake in the oven for 15 minutes or less. Be careful not to brown them too much.

GALANI O CHIACCHIERE
FRIED SWEET PASTRIES

This is fried pastry used at carnival time. There are many variations on the same theme, the difference being in the lightness of the outcome. I find this pastry useful for coffee or to accompany a creamy dessert like crème brûlée *or a* zabaglione. *The word* galani *comes from* gale, *Venetian for 'ribbon'.*

For a nice pile
PREPARATION TIME: 1 HOUR
3 cups plain (all-purpose) flour
a pinch of baking soda
3/4 cup sugar
5 eggs
7 tablespoons butter, softened
a nip of Grand Marnier
grated zest of an orange
oil for frying
icing (confectioners) sugar

Place the flour, baking soda and sugar in a bowl. Make a hole in the centre and add the eggs, butter, liqueur and orange zest. Mix into smooth dough and then allow the pastry to rest in a cool place for 30 minutes. Then roll it out on a floured surface with a rolling pin or a pasta machine to a thickness of 3 mm (1/8 inch). Cut the pastry into short ribbons or tie up in dainty knots.

Roll out only a few at a time before frying in clean oil until golden. This is to stop the pastry drying out. When fried, dust with icing sugar.

Biscotti di Mandorla
Almond Biscuits

Like the galani (on page 211), there are infinite variations on this classic biscuit. This biscotto is designed to partner a good caffè espresso, soft dessert or ice-cream. This recipe is so simple that even kids can have a go at baking it.

Makes a large pile
PREPARATION TIME: 10 MINUTES
BAKING TIME: 25 MINUTES,
DEPENDING ON OVEN

3 cups self-raising flour

1 cup slivered almonds
(can be browned in the oven)

125 mL (½ cup) olive oil

5 eggs

1 cup sugar

a pinch of salt

a nip of brandy, Amaretto or another liqueur

Preheat the oven to 180°C (350°F).

Combine all the ingredients in a bowl. Divide the mixture into 4 logs of 3–4 cm (1 ½ in) diameter. Place on a tray covered with baking paper, sprinkle with sugar and place in the oven.

When the logs have browned a little and have stiffened like bread — after 20 minutes or so — remove them from the oven and cool.

When completely cold cut them at an angle into 5 mm (¼ in) slices. Place the biscuits on the baking tray and back into the oven until they change colour. If you leave them too long they'll dry out too much for my taste. But then they are wonderful with sticky wine or *vin santo*, the fortified wine of Tuscany.

INDEX OF RECIPES

DOLCI E BISCOTTI
SWEETS AND BISCUITS

INDEX